T0243630

OKAY,
NOW
WHAT?

OKAY, NOW WHAT?

HOW TO BE RESILIENT WHEN LIFE *GETS TOUGH*

KATE GLADDIN

alcove
press

To Mum and Dad,
for your endless strength and support
no matter what life throws our way.
I love you both dearly.

CONTENTS

INTRODUCTION

Why Resilience Matters

"She didn't make it."

You know those moments in life that are so defining that you almost feel like a stranger to the person you were before it happened? This was that moment for me, the moment my Mum said:

"She didn't make it."

Maybe you're thinking, "Oh, she must not have made it into college," or "She didn't make it through the interview process." No, my Mum was telling me she didn't make it through surgery.

"She" is my sister. And she didn't make it.

I don't know which moments from your own life just came to mind as you read this, but I'm guessing if this book is in your hand, it's because you've been blindsided by life, too. Perhaps you have also lost someone you love, or maybe you're coping with your career plans getting derailed, or your "happily ever after" ending abruptly. Whatever you've been through, you may have discovered—as I have—that the only certainty in life is change. And for many of us, this change can be unwanted and come at a huge loss.

Whether it's loss of opportunity, loss of health, loss of relationships, loss of financial security, or simply loss of expectation, life involves loss, change, and pain. There's no getting around it; there's only getting through it. You may have heard the saying, "What doesn't kill us makes us stronger," yet you may have noticed that's not the case for everyone. Some people do become a shell of who they used to be or seem to stay stuck in a place of blame or resentment at the world when they're dealt an unfair card in life, while other people do really seem to transform their hardships into opportunities for growth and bettering themselves.

The difference between the two is *resilience*. Resilience is your capacity to adapt to unexpected change, manage your stress in the face of adversity, and move forward from your losses in a positive way.

While school and college taught me how to be many things—smarter, more tech savvy, a better marketer—it did not teach me anything about how to be resilient. In fact, college-age me was the complete opposite of resilient; a bad exam grade or someone else's negative opinion of me used to crush me. I was constantly on an emotional roller coaster and mentally fragile at best. I've come a long way in building up my own resilience. Resilience isn't a fixed trait about you, like your eye color or the shape of your toes. Resilience is a skillset that any of us can grow and develop with practice. So if you also struggle with spiraling into anxiety and are overwhelmed when life hits you with a setback, or you're feeling completely lost in a fog after your world was turned upside down, then stick with me. I promise you, who you've been and where you are right now isn't where you have to stay. In fact, transition and change can be an amazing catalyst for growth.

Before we start, I want to tell you more about my story. Because if I'm going to write a whole book about resilience, I want you to know that I understand how helpless life can leave you feeling.

October 20, 2012. That's the day my world as I knew it was shattered.

I was 20 years old, and I remember going to bed the night before, feeling stressed about university exams and what I was going to wear to my friend's party the next day (because you know, if your outfit isn't on point—then what's the point?!). Little did I know that I was only hours away from a life-changing turning point.

I woke up to my phone buzzing beside me. My alarm clock said it was 3:37 AM. Immediately I thought, "seriously?! Who calls at this hour?! It's got to be a friend doing a prank." But I grabbed my phone and realized it was no prank—it was my Mum. She sounded a bit worried and asked if I knew my sister's email password. My sister was on holiday in Thailand and needed her travel insurance documents. So I sleepily opened my laptop, broke into her email (as only a younger sister can do), and forwarded it to Mum. I really didn't think much about it—but then Mum's voice broke and she said, "Nicole's been in an accident, pray to God she's OK."

I was stunned. Speechless. Nicole was four years older than me. I quite literally couldn't imagine life without her in it, because she'd always been there. I used to wake up to the sound of her tapping her feet on our kitchen floor. She was born a dancer and could never keep her feet still. She felt everything deeply. One time, she cried when our dog came home with a really bad haircut!

After that call, I was praying I'd see her again. I walked down to the beach to clear my head, but it was impossible. My mind was racing with thoughts: "*How did this happen? Whose fault was it? Is she really going to be OK?!*"

As I looked up at the most stunning sunrise rising over the ocean, I thought, "Oh, *look at that! This is a sign! Look how beautiful this is. It's a sign she's going to be OK!*" I pulled out my phone and took a photo to show Nicole when I would go to visit her in the hospital. Because I was convinced she was going to be fine.

I walked shakily toward my car to drive to my parent's house. I knew they needed me—but I couldn't bear the thought of facing them, of seeing their panic-stricken faces and the fear in their eyes.

That would suddenly make this real, and I didn't want this to be real. I took one last deep breath before I sank into the driver's seat. I hadn't even closed my door yet when my phone started ringing—Mum again.

I told myself not to panic, thinking she probably wanted me to pick up milk on the way home or something. I swiped to answer, and all I heard was Mum scream, "She didn't make it." I dropped my phone, collapsed onto the grass, and wailed at the top of my lungs.

When I arrived at my family home, I saw it was already filled with people giving their condolences. I wanted to scream "Get out, leave us alone!" but I knew they were only trying to help. I found my way into my Mum's arms and we both collapsed, sobbing. She pulled away from me and said "Katie, I need you to take a deep breath and look at me. Your Dad and I have a flight booked for Thailand to recover Nicole's body, and it's leaving in 30 minutes."

Minutes later, I gave Mum and Dad one last hug before they left for the airport. Releasing that hug was the hardest thing I've had to do.

Over a glitchy Skype call, my Dad told me what happened after seeing video footage of the accident from the hotel camera in Koh Samui: Nicole and her boyfriend, Jaime, were on a motorbike turning into the driveway of their hotel when another driver on the wrong side of the road slammed into them. "We've spent a day in the police station negotiating with the police," he said. "They've taken Jamie's passport, and the driver is not at all sorry for what happened."

"What do you mean 'negotiating' with the police?" My sister was dead, and now I had to worry about whether Nicole's boyfriend would end up in a Thai prison.

After a few more sleepless nights, long days of crying on my bathroom floor and using every tissue we had, we finally got the call that they were all coming home. The next few weeks were a blur. I picked out Nicole's burial dress. I wrote a speech for her memorial. Three thousand people showed up, and I wondered, "If I died, would I inspire so many people to come to my funeral?"

A few days after Nicole's memorial service, I wandered into a cafe. Still half asleep and waiting for coffee to brew, I casually looked up at the TV. I saw blurry footage of a couple on a motorbike. As the other bike sped toward them, it dawned on me. *Hang on second, that's my sister!* I thought. I was watching the moment of my sister's death on TV in a cafe.

I had no idea how I was going to make it through the grief. It felt like things just kept getting worse, and there was nothing I could do to fix it or make it all go away. I felt completely helpless.

You might be reading this book because you're going through a time in your life when you're feeling the same way. Maybe your mother has sat you down and told you her doctor found a lump— she has cancer. Or your boss has given the promotion you worked so hard for to the colleague who's been using all of your ideas without giving you any credit. Or you've found texts on your boyfriend's phone and realized he hasn't really been "working late" after all.

When you're blindsided by a situation you have no control over, it feels like blame and anger is pulsing through every part of you. I get it. Initially, I couldn't stop thinking about the driver who killed my sister. I despised him. I could not believe that he got away with it. That the police never properly charged him. That he didn't even seem to care. The blame and bitterness crippled me. Perhaps your blame is keeping you stuck also, but you're not even sure what the first steps forward look like.

In this book, I'll take you through the powerful strategy I developed from discovering insights that finally helped me to stop dwelling on the injustice of my sister's death and the intense negative emotions surrounding it, so I was able to get my power back over my response. This book will go beyond the stereotypical self-help advice of "just look on the bright side" when you're struggling. Sure, a motivational quote can brighten your day a little and positive thinking has its merits, but when I was lying on the floor of my sister's closet trying to pick a dress for her to be buried in, positivity was not at all helpful or what I needed. I needed something to help me heal my pain, not pretend it wasn't there. This book isn't about turning you into a robot who feels positive all the time. It's about helping you understand *why* you feel what you feel and how you can influence those emotions in more helpful and healing ways.

To do this, I'll introduce my innovative 3 R strategy to resilience: *Recognize* your thoughts, *Reflect* on how your thoughts impact you, and *Redirect* your mind to more empowering thoughts. This is how I turned my shitty circumstance into a career that's impacted thousands of lives for the better. Now I want the same transformation for you. To help you build your resilience and gain back control over your response to life, even in moments where everything feels upside down and inside out.

I believe in the power of what I'm going to teach you, because I've used this strategy not only to grow through the grief of losing my sister, but so much more. At 20 years old, it gave me the courage to quit my corporate job so I could become the director of my sister's charity, the Nicole Fitzsimons Foundation. The decision made little financial sense—I wasn't getting paid for the director's role. But I had a vision to make a difference in honor of my sister and try to save others from her tragic fate. So, I created a travel safety presentation that I delivered to over 200,000 students at schools around Australia and even had the opportunity to speak at government events alongside the Australian Foreign Minister. I would've never had the guts to pursue that dream—especially with everyone thinking I was *crazy* for walking away from my corporate career—without understanding the 3 Rs I'll teach you in this book.

The road to achieving this goal with my sister's charity was not easy. In the first year, I sent out 600 emails to schools to speak with their students and only eight booked me in. That's 592 rejections. But the 3 Rs kept me going on the days when quitting was tempting and progress was slow. My travel safety mission soon evolved into a resilience and mental health mission for young people. I created my own presentation to teach students everything I've learned about resilience, because I struggled so much with it as a teen myself. I was scared to make this change and let go of working full time on my sister's charity. But I went all in and took a loan from my Dad to go to a program in the United States to become a life coach at the age of 24. By the end of the following year, I was invited to speak at schools in the United States, which was so well received that I began to get invited back more and more. So began the challenge of setting up my company in a foreign country, a process so complicated I constantly felt in way over my head. I now run a six-figure coaching company on my own here in the United States, but boy oh boy, some days felt—and still feel—like I'm climbing up a mountain with blocks of concrete on my feet.

In my twenties, I also went through difficult break-ups and ended up in a relationship that felt very safe to me but also unfulfilling. He was a great guy who ticked all the boxes on paper, but in my heart, that thrill of true love wasn't there. People close to me judged me for wanting to leave him and thought I was being selfish. But having buried my sister at 20 years old, I knew life was too short to settle, especially when it came to love. So, the 3 Rs made me brave enough to once again make a decision that scared me but that I knew deep down was the best decision—for both of us. He deserved to find his true love, too. Soon after that, I was swept off my feet by an incredible man named Nate whom I met while I was on vacation in the United States. We fell in love, and I eventually got my visa to live with him here in the United States.

Oh, but then that thing called the pandemic decided to blind-side the world. I know we *all* have a story of how life was turned upside down when Covid set in, and 2020 will forever be the year the world learned just how quickly life can change. While I was able to come to the United States to start my life with Nate, it ended up being nearly two years until I could visit my family in Australia. We have an amazing relationship and a way of bringing out the best in each other, but I will admit that first year was rough. Nate was in the Air Force and spent more time away than he did at home. Neighbors were still standoffish from Covid, and I struggled to make friends. On top of that, I couldn't go out and do what I loved most—speak at schools and events—because group gatherings were still a no-go. I felt lonely and isolated, but I was able to work through that struggle thanks to the 3 Rs, which helped me open up to difficult conversations and decisions that had to be made. I am so thankful to my past self now for not giving up. I can't imagine not living the incredible life I now have.

Even though I've achieved such success, I continue to fall on my face. I still need to call a friend to vent about work stress or cry on the couch with my dog on a tough day. I'm still human, therefore I still struggle, but I no longer feel completely stuck at the effect of what's happening in my life. I know how to control my responses in a way that helps me move through my challenges rather than wallow in them. That has changed my whole experience in this messy world. And now I'm excited to teach you the same steps so you can experience the difference it makes in your life.

Throughout this book, you'll notice there are exercises and journal prompts to help you put what you're learning in this book into practice. You're welcome to use your own journal to answer those questions. Additionally, to make answering them even easier for you to do, I've created free mini e-book with some of these worksheets and journal pages all ready for you to complete! You can download it by scanning this QR code. You'll also find this QR code throughout the book, next to the activities that I've created a complimentary online resource for, so be sure to take advantage of that extra support.

We're going to cover a lot of ground together, so if you're like me and want to make sure the stuff that really hits home stays with you, you can also grab a journal to jot down notes or a highlighter to highlight the parts you really find helpful. Life happens fast, so it's great to be able to quickly refer back to these tips and strategies when you need them most!

Together, let's take our next steps toward becoming more resilient.

PART I

Understanding
The Power of Resilience

I

What Is Resilience?

When I moved to the United States in the summer of 2020, my awesome then-5-year-old nephew would FaceTime my now husband, Nate, and me. The most fun part of all was never knowing if he'd appear on the screen wearing a Batman suit or a Captain America one (Nate being the proud American he is, was always hoping for the latter!). Seeing my nephew dressed up like a superhero was adorable, and we loved how much fun he was having.

You also may remember dressing up like a superhero for playtime or Halloween when you were a kid. I mean, who doesn't want to be strong and powerful enough to always save the day?! It's all fun and games when we're young. But now as an adult, trying to be invincible against the pain and loss of everyday life can be crippling to our ability to actually cope with it.

Unfortunately, many people misconceive being resilient as never letting anything in life bring you down. They might say things like, "Just be happy, and don't let things worry you." This approach to life is about as realistic as the Hulk's ability to turn green. Humans are feeling creatures, and feelings are complex. You can't just flash your cape around a few times and make them disappear. And you certainly can't outrun them—and yet so many of us often try to. And I can't blame anyone who does. I know I used to.

I graduated from school knowing how to solve an algebra equation or write an essay, but I still hadn't learned *how* to be resilient—or what that term even means. The few times I did hear the word "resilience" thrown around at school, I remember it being explained to me as bouncing back after life knocks you down. Perhaps you've heard a similar explanation before. On the surface, there's nothing wrong with thinking of it that way. However, take a moment to think about the last time you were hit with something painful or unexpected in life. Did you instantly and effortlessly bounce back the next minute? The next hour? The next day?

Unfortunately, it's not realistic to bounce back instantly from a tragedy like a basketball bouncing back up from the ground. We're not elastic bands that can snap back to happiness. Yet, if we think that's what resilience is, we'll constantly feel like we're failing at it. And that self-judgment only makes things ten times harder to cope. That's why getting clear on what resilience *really* is, is so important. If we're not being realistic about what it means to be human, "humaning" only gets harder!

So instead of thinking of resilience as bouncing or smothering your struggle with smiles, think of resilience as being about building a set of skills to help you face the world with courage, adapt to change, and become mentally stronger—not in spite of your challenges, but because of them. At the core of being able to do all of these things is your ability to control your response to life. This is why I developed my 3 Rs; they're here to give you the framework you need to build resilience by learning how to respond on purpose, not just react by default.

Think of resilience as being about building a set of skills to help you face the world with courage, adapt to change, and become mentally stronger.

Nothing about this is instant or easy. Rather, it's a practice, one that is as straightforward as toddlers doodling with a marker on the wall. Some days you may feel like you have it together, and you're finally adulting—maybe you've finally stopped texting your toxic ex or stopped melting down over a snide remark from your coworker. You feel in control and ready to face whatever comes your way. Then, life blindsides you and you're left needing to curl back up for a good cry and drown yourself in reruns of *Friends*. And the interesting thing is, when I say life "blindsides you," I'm not just talking about the big moments where you receive a life-changing diagnosis or discover your fiancé has been sleeping with his assistant. There can be things that are seemingly simple on the surface, but if past wounds and insecurities haven't been healed, little things become big things, and our reaction to it is like a tidal wave crashing over a stone. In these cases, we often react way out of proportion to what's really going on.

For example, whenever I used to lose a tennis match that I was initially winning, I felt moody and reactive to anyone else who was around me for the rest of the day. That's because losing triggered so much inner turmoil for me. Resilience for these everyday moments is just as important as resilience for the heart-wrenching moments. We need to learn how to keep mole hills as mole hills, and use those experiences as training for when life really does put a mountain in front of us that we're forced to climb.

Recently I was working with a woman called Bella, who was going through a divorce after her husband cheated on her. She showed up on Zoom looking completely exhausted, sitting on her bedroom floor surrounded by boxes and suitcases. Part of coaching is being a safe space for someone to let out all of their thoughts and feelings, so I listened as she started venting about how much she hated him for what he's putting her through but even more so, how much she hated herself. "How did I not see this coming? Why am I so stupid that I ever trusted him? What's wrong with me?" With glassy eyes looking back at me, I could see she felt completely helpless.

Out of all the feelings in the world, I think helplessness is the one that causes us to struggle the most. No one wants to feel like their emotions are at the mercy of all the random and unpredictable things that can happen in daily life. Roller coasters are great in theme parks, but they're not so great when it comes to our emotional lives. And yet without the skill of resilience, that's how it feels: when things are going your way—like the sun is shining, your boss thinks you're great, and your boyfriend compliments how amazing you look—life feels lighter and more manageable, like you really are the CEO of your own life. But as soon as life starts throwing you some curveballs—maybe you miss the bus to work, your computer crashes before you save an important document, or you're being ghosted by yet another online date—it's so easy to let your emotions run away into self pity, frustration and helplessness. Next thing you know we're picking a fight with our partner, snapping at the poor worker at the checkout, and canceling going to our friend's birthday dinner.

Resilience is actually a lot like brushing your teeth. Brushing our teeth is something we need to do daily, and even though we cleaned them the night before, the next day we still need to give them a good scrub because of the food and bacteria that builds up in between. Same goes with our resilience; it's not a one-time thing, it's a daily practice, because life keeps coming at us daily. Even though you may have been able to pep talk your way through a tense moment with your boss without losing your temper, it doesn't mean that you won't need to practice the same cognitive skills the next time she's telling you off again. Resilience isn't a destination you arrive at where you're going to be totally Zen and at peace with everything that's happening in your life 24/7, resilience is more of a skillset you put into practice throughout every step of your journey in life.

I'm speaking from experience here; I know how tough life feels when you're lacking in mental and emotional resilience. That's why I'm so passionate about helping you build it. Even as a resilience coach, I still have days where I lie in my closet and have a good cry because it feels dark and safe away from the rest of the world. I still need to vent to my husband about the stress of life or the emptiness I feel for moments I wish my sister could've been there to share with me. I still feel all the "feels" that come with being human. The difference is that I no longer feel helpless over supporting myself through those emotions. I understand the steps I need to take to process through these feelings rather than spiral into them. Now I want the same for you, to feel like you're in the driver's seat of your life experience, not the passenger on a Wild West roller coaster that has you scrambling for sanity.

Resilience ultimately takes practice, patience, and perseverance—oh, and a good sense of humor helps, too! In the following pages I've stripped it all back to share with you the most meaningful and eye-opening lessons, tools, and insights I learned to help end my sense of helplessness once and for all. Once you know how to harness the power of your response, your life will never be the same again.

2

What Holds Us Back

One cold winter's morning on my way to the gym, I was trying to pull the protective cover off the middle console of my car with absolutely no success. I was getting all frazzled about it. I'm sure it would've been highly amusing to watch. What I didn't realize was that there was an extra elastic piece I needed to release before the cover would slide off. This experience reminds me of any new change we're trying to make—it's not just what you need to do next; it's about what you need to *stop* doing that's been keeping you stuck.

When it comes to life knocking us down, there are things we need to give up before we're able to get up. That's what this chapter is all about. I'll call out the unhelpful habits and things we do that keep us digging further into the ditch of struggle and misery. These four habits are the main things that rob us of our resilience: blaming, shaming, resisting, and escaping.

This chapter might not be the most comfortable chapter for you to read, as it's going to involve taking a real look at your own life. But I have one request: please do this self-reflection from a place of compassion and curiosity. I'm not pointing these things out for you to then beat yourself up about them. I'm doing it because we can't change what we're not aware of. We need to begin to see the ways we're sabotaging ourselves or making things harder so we can understand *why* we need to stop doing these things.

I'm not here to lie to you: changing ourselves and habits of behavior ain't easy. It can be tempting to stick your head in the sand or justify away why you do some of these things to try and cope. But once you begin to see how they perpetuate your struggle rather than help you cope, it does help spark that commitment to stop doing those things. When you partner up commitment with compassion, you can simply evaluate your habits as helpful or unhelpful; with the unhelpful habits being those things that may feel good in the moment but can be most harmful to us long term.

The reason I don't want you to get self-critical about any habits you realize are unhelpful, is because we're all just doing the best we can to keep our heads above water some days. That means we tend to cling on to whatever feels like it's going to get us through those moments. So I'm not saying that it's *wrong* to blame, shame, resist, or escape, or that you're *weak* if you do them. In fact, we *all* do them sometimes, because "humaning" can be freaking hard. But I do want to highlight to you the ways in which these habits and choices are about as useful as hiking with rocks in your backpack. The rocks are only going to make the climb to the top harder, tire you out quicker, and provide no additional energy or strength.

Let's dig a little more into what blaming, shaming, resisting, and escaping really are, and why they're things we need to stop doing in order to be more resilient. As we go through each of them, take a moment to think about whether it's a reaction or habit you tend to default to and how its effects have played out in your life.

Blaming

I don't think many of us like to admit we play the "blame game," but we all do it from time to time. It's when you point your finger at someone and blame them for your problems or why your life is such a struggle or in a bad place. And sometimes this blame seems very justified, especially if someone has done something that has a direct impact on you and your circumstances. Like my with client, Bella. She was blaming her husband for ruining their marriage and derailing what she thought would be their happily-ever-after together. On the surface, it makes sense that she's blaming him for all the damage he'd caused in her life.

I know I certainly felt justified for blaming the driver for ruining my family's life the day he hit my sister on his motorbike and took her away from us forever. I remember sitting on the edge of my bed the day I found out about her death, closing my eyes and trying to picture myself as a 60-year-old woman saying "It's been 40 years since I've seen my sister." I just couldn't picture it. I couldn't comprehend how he could steal away the future I had with my sister or how I'd ever be happy again without her in my life. I hated him with every vein in my body.

Who is that person that you feel is to blame for messing up your life in some way? Or maybe it's not a person, but an event—an incident that sent your world spinning. I know a family whose home was ruined by a flood, one friend whose brother was diagnosed with a rare cancer, and another friend whose mother *and* father died before my friend was 16 years old. The biggest difference I noticed about how well they were able to get through these things is whether or not they get caught up in the blame game.

When something first happens, and we're in a lot of pain, shock or grief, it makes sense to take all of our emotions out on that person or the world for what's happened. The world is filled with unpredictable disasters and people who have cruel intentions, and these events or people really are to blame for their actions and the immediate impacts those actions have on you. For example, if a driver is texting at a traffic light and hits the back of your car, she is responsible for damaging your vehicle, the bruise on your forehead, and you being late to your first meeting. Her actions are her responsibility. But the truth is that how much that event impacts the rest of your day and how you feel about it emotionally in the long term is not her fault.

When you think your boss, your brother, your friend, your coworker, the weather, or any other random force is to blame for what happened and why you're now struggling so much, you give away all of your power because they're all things we cannot control. And that's where helplessness comes from: believing that something outside of our control is to blame for why our lives are the way they are or why we feel the way we feel. So *Blaming breeds self-pity, rumination, and bitterness: the complete opposite of what we need to fuel resilience.* while blaming may feel powerful in the moment, in the long term, it's a jail cell. Blaming breeds self-pity, rumination, and bitterness: the complete opposite of what we need to fuel resilience.

Shaming

Like peanut butter and jelly (or vegemite and cheese for my Aussies!), blaming and shaming often go hand in hand. The difference is that with shaming, we're directing the blame toward ourselves. I see this a lot when it comes to regretting a past choice or for taking a risk in some way that doesn't pay off.

I've had coaching clients come to me shaming themselves for all kinds of reasons, from having a panic attack in the middle of a marketing presentation to sleeping through an alarm and missing their flight to their friend's birthday getaway. Shaming self-talk sounds like, "You idiot, why did you do that?!" or "You should've known better!" or "What's wrong with you?!"

When heartbroken Bella wasn't spinning over blame and anger at her ex-husband, she was quick to go to the other extreme of shaming herself for missing years of red flags in her marriage. When they were getting married, her own best friend was even trying to talk her out of the marriage days before the wedding because she could sense this guy wasn't as genuine as he seemed. He'd shower Bella with designer gifts and vacations, but then ghost her while he was on business trips and make her feel bad for questioning his lack of contact. In hindsight, she could see what a red flag that was, but at the time, she was completely besotted with this guy. She stopped returning her friends' calls and began isolating herself from her friend group. She stopped going out with anyone other than him and would wait up at night for him to call her after work—sometimes he did, other times he'd just ignore her. When she'd get upset, he'd say all the right things to make her feel he really did love her deeply. The next day, the cycle started all over again.

Thankfully, through our work together in coaching sessions, Bella began to see what an unhealthy marriage she was in, which all came to a head when she discovered texts that exposed his infidelity with other women while he was on work trips. She found the courage to end their marriage, which she initially felt really good about. But then she was spiraling into shame about how she let herself get into such a toxic relationship in the first place and how she couldn't see through all of his lies that looking back now were so obvious to her. She sat in front of me, with her head buried in her hands, crying and mumbling, "How could I be so blind to miss what was right in front of me? Maybe I don't deserve anything better than this for being so foolish in the first place!"

Shaming comes from placing expectations on ourselves that we should *never* make mistakes and *always* be able to anticipate any potential threats or misfortunes ahead of time so we can avoid them at all costs. Expecting perfection from yourself is unrealistic and being able to predict the future is only something you'll find in a sci-fi movie. Yet when something bad happens, it's easy to beat ourselves up for it and stay caught up in the "coulda, shoulda, wouldas."

I even did this with my sister's death. When I wasn't busy blaming the other driver for what happened, I started blaming myself for it. Yes that's right, I was thousands of miles away from the scene of the accident, but still I felt a huge rush of shame burn hot in my chest when I remembered I was the one who suggested Nicole visit Thailand. She initially wasn't sure where she wanted to go on vacation, and we used to share our thoughts about everything, so off she went to Thailand upon my suggestion. I cannot tell you how much I wanted to shake and scream at my past self for doing that. *"Why didn't I just keep my mouth shut?!"* I thought. *"She never would've been in Thailand if it weren't for me."*

It's crazy how much we want to feel like we can control the world, that we'll try to find any way we can to link an incident back to us and our choices—as if we have that much power over what happens out there in the universe. It's easier to take fault for what happened than to admit we do live in an unpredictable world that is beyond our control. At least that's why I think my psyche spiraled into that shame and blame over my sister's death. And it's also why you might be doing the same over something that's happened in your life, whether there's a direct link between your actions and the outcome or there's a very vague and convoluted way to link your actions to what happened, like with my sister's death. I know that beating yourself up for past choices feels tempting and somewhat necessary, as though if you just hate yourself enough, you might be able to undo what happened.

The truth is that the opposite is true. The self-loathing and helplessness that shame creates makes things even worse. It makes us lash out in ways that cause more harm than good. Shames perpetuates shame.

The other big problem about shame is that it keeps us from healing the wounds and emotions beneath it. When we're focused on who's to blame for what happened, whether it's ourselves or others, we're not really processing the emotions that will naturally come up as a result of loss or hardship. We're so busy assigning fault that we're not really *feeling* what needs to be felt in order to begin to heal and grow from it.

Shaming yourself only makes you sink further into helplessness. Because no matter how loudly you and Cher can sing, "If I could turn back time," none of us have the power to do so. I can't go back and tell my sister not to go to Thailand. You can't rewind and start your job interview over. You can't rewrite your story so you never fall for the temptation to kiss your married coworker. Yes that's right, I am also writing this book for people who know it's because of their own less-than-wise choices that there's hardship in their life.

If this is you—if you've done something that you regret because of the pain and suffering it's caused yourself and others—I want to help you see you still don't need to keep yourself locked in a hidden prison of shame. It's crippling and starving your resilience of oxygen. The challenges that exist in our lives because of our past mistakes are experiences that we do need to learn from, but you'll never be able to grow from a place of shame. That's what I had to help Bella see to envision a better path, because otherwise she was going to go back into that toxic place of pushing everyone away from her again because she felt so unworthy. Shame perpetuates unworthiness, which leads to us shutting down and hiding away from friends and family during the exact moments we need them most. So as much as you could prove to me why whatever happened is your fault, continually torturing yourself over it is not serving you or any of the relationships in your life.

Resisting

"It just shouldn't have happened the way it did. It wasn't supposed to be this way."

If you want to find the quickest way to disempower yourself, it's arguing against your current reality. I could argue all day long about how my sister should still be alive, but it's not going to make any difference. She's never coming back and me continually begging for her to return only zaps me of my own resilience. The same goes for whatever thing you're insisting should be different about your past or present. It's about as helpful as shouting at the tide of the ocean to stop coming in. You can present to me the most logical and well thought out argument about why the tide should be different, but it's still going to do what it does regardless. You cannot control it. The same goes with your past. It's as over as Ancient Rome.

Yet so many of us get caught in the spiral of ruminating over what we think shouldn't have happened, as if somehow we can change it. I sadly experienced this with a friend who went through a divorce after he was caught gambling away their money and lying to his wife about it. It was hard on everyone involved, and he'd call me up constantly to talk about it. I was happy to help, especially because I did not want him going through his struggle alone. However, every time we talked, he'd spin into the same frenzy of resistance, saying things like, "I can win her back. She doesn't really want this divorce. It doesn't have to be this way." The reality was that his wife had no interest in reconciling, but my friend also had no interest in accepting her decision. And it made him spiral into a very bad place. He stopped sleeping and eating properly, and would relentlessly try to reach out to his ex, which made things even messier and more emotional. He refused to accept her decision, thinking he could fight it, but the fight was already over. His ex-wife had moved on. And by living in denial of it, he lost all ability to be resilient and learn from his mistakes.

Pay attention to the sneaky ways you might be resisting your reality. You'll know you're in a place of resistance if you're "shoulding" over a situation, like "My Mom is such a sweet person, she shouldn't have cancer" or "My coworker shouldn't have gotten that promotion, they don't deserve it." No matter how unfair your current circumstances may seem to you, there's zero upside to fighting against them. We only get so much mental energy in a day, and it makes no sense to waste it all on things we cannot control.

Escaping

Thanks to today's technology and the never ending availability of pleasure and fun we have at our fingertips, escaping our emotions through distractions has become one of the easiest ways to try and cope with how we feel. I'm talking about things like endlessly scrolling social media, vaping in the toilets at work, inhaling a bottle of wine after work every night, skipping the gym to get a supersized pizza and tub of ice cream to match. All of these things are what I call "dopamine bombs"—they'll instantly flood you with an overload of the brain's feel good chemical, dopamine, that numbs out how you're really feeling. It makes sense why we do it; we're a species wired to seek out states of pleasure and avoid discomfort. So if there's an easy way to step out of the pain or uncomfortable emotions of our current reality, our instinct will be to do so.

What's interesting is that it's not just binge eating or overdoing things like online shopping that can be an escape mechanism for our emotions. Even things that are considered healthy can become a vice. For example, exercising a lot and eating a little can look healthy on the surface, but when it's in a very restrictive and controlled manner, it can be just as detrimental as any other escape mechanism we're using. When I was in high school, trying to escape my own sense of helplessness led to me developing disordered eating tendencies and starving myself. I remember hating how little control it felt like I had when I finished up school that I began to try to seek control through food. I became obsessed with what I ate and weighed, to the point I remember sitting down trying to study for my final exams but I'd feel a wave of anxiety come over me and I'd instantly go weigh myself to try relieve it because seeing the number go down on the scale and know I caused that gave me some sense of control. If you are reading this and feel that you too are displaying these disordered eating behaviors, please seek professional help as soon as possible—there are resources listed at the back of this book.

The biggest problem with my controlled eating was, just like everything we do to try to escape how we're feeling or our current reality, the relief was as temporary as the distraction itself. On the other side of escapism, once the dopamine high wears off, we're left feeling just as helpless as we did before and usually with more negative consequences. I'm not against taking time out to veg out on the couch with a glass of wine to watch your favorite show or enjoy a few cute puppy reels to brighten your day. Taking time to unwind and relax is important for mental health, and we all have different ways of doing that, but when we're using that as a way to constantly avoid dealing with what's going on in our lives or how we're feeling, it's a slippery slope that can unfortunately lead to issues like addiction and depression. Feelings are made to be felt, not avoided. Trying to do the latter is a losing battle.

Ending the Cycle

Well, I warned you the majority of this chapter wasn't going to be the easiest read. Whether you're caught up in blame, shame, resistance, or doing your best to escape it all, I want you to remember, it's a common cycle. You are not alone. My hand is extended for you to grab a hold of, because together I promise we're going to break this cycle.

The first step is acknowledging and reflecting on which of these coping mechanisms you have perhaps been falling into and how that's been impacting you personally. Remember, we do these exercises to raise our awareness of what we'd like to begin to change, not to judge ourselves for what we've been doing. There's no right or wrong, there's just helpful or unhelpful. Read through your answers as if your friend wrote them so you look over them with compassionate rather than critical eyes.

Grab a journal and pen, or open up a note section in your phone, and answer the following prompts:

1. Make a list of people who you think are to blame for your current problems in life and why. Don't edit yourself here—just let it all come out as if you're venting to a friend.
2. What can you control or change about this person to make the situation better? (*Hint* We can't control other people, no matter how hard we try!)
3. How does it feel to blame something you can't control for how you feel?

4. Which problems do you have in life that you think are all your fault? Why do you believe they are your fault?

5. When you blame or shame yourself in this way, what do you do to try and cope with those feelings? *(It may be to hide away and not be as social, nitpick yourself in the mirror, text the ex who you know is no good for you, skip doing your self-care routine, etc.)*

6. What are things that you notice you do when you're trying to escape or numb out feelings that you don't want to feel? How do you typically feel after doing those things—better or worse?

7. If you could learn how to feel better without relying on those coping mechanisms or escapisms, how could your life be better?

Breaking the cycle won't be easy, because blaming, shaming, and denying reality is a typical knee-jerk reaction a lot of society has to the hard things that happen in our lives. But it's worth the effort of unlearning these habits of behavior, because they all lead you down a one-way street to feeling even more bitter and helpless over why your life is the way it is.

That is why I'm writing this book for you. Because I want you to stop feeling like you're on that exhausting roller coaster just living with the effect of what's happening in your life. I want you to stop feeling helpless. I want you to *live* your best life, even if the unthinkable shatters your world as you know it. And that begins the moment you learn that there is another way forward. In the following chapters, I will teach you my 3 R strategy to show you step by step the choices you can make instead to gain back control of your life. Not to dismiss or minimize your struggle or loss as if they don't matter, but to show you how to turn those experiences into something more: something purposeful, something growth worthy, and something that makes you fall back in love with life again.

If you are going through a time in your life where you are reaching out and yearning for things to be different in ways that you can't control, I am writing this book for you, too. I assure you that after learning and applying what you learn in this book, you will never struggle with this same sense of helplessness again.

3

From Blame to Response-Ability

I'd just finished giving a travel safety presentation to a group of hundreds of students, when one student's hand shot up. She curiously asked me, "How did you get past the anger and bitterness over what happened in your sister's accident?"

I've written this book to answer that exact question. Because if I had a dollar for every time a student had asked me a question like that, I'd be able to buy my dog an endless supply of his favorite bones.

The most heartbreaking part of that question is when students would follow it up by saying, "I'd never be able to be so strong." Of all the things that have motivated me to be on the path I am on today, those words have definitely been the most impactful. I didn't grow up naturally resilient. I was reactive and emotional and easily frustrated by the simplest things not going my way. And if you had told my younger self that I would lose my sister to an accident, I would've told you I'd never get up off the bathroom floor. I couldn't comprehend ever going through such a tragedy and finding a way to cope. Not only was I hit with the loss of one of the closest people in the world to me, my family also had to navigate a very biased justice system that led to the other driver not being properly charged for my sister's death. It all felt too incomprehensible and during those first few days after she passed away, it didn't even feel real. In between the uncontrollable sobbing of tears and mountains of tissues, I was waiting for someone to wake me up from a really bad dream. This could not be my life now. Things like this didn't happen to my family. There must have be some sort of mistake.

But as the reality of it all began to sink in, the shock gave way to anger and bitterness. How could the world be so cruel as to take away the person whom I'd brushed my teeth next to every day and shared my favorite pair of jeans with? You expect to lose your parents one day in the natural cycle of life. But your sibling? It's not the way life is supposed to go. My sister was supposed to one day be my maid of honor and squeal with excitement while helping me choose my wedding dress. I've realized that when you lose someone you love, you don't just grieve the moments that are now memories. You also grieve all the future moments that you know will never get to become memories.

I was beginning to spiral into a dark fog of grief, sometimes so thick it would steal the air from me. I didn't want to know a world without my sister. I didn't want to accept this new reality. I'd lie on the bathroom floor where we'd get ready together each day and silently beg for the universe to find a way to turn back time, to bring Nicole home, to let me take her place. But I couldn't. I couldn't do anything to undo the moments that stole away my sister and my life as I knew it. I felt completely helpless. And alone. Not many 20-year olds have gone through trauma like this—not any of my friends at least. They sent me their condolences over text and came along to Nicole's memorial. But besides that, their contact with me was scarce. In hindsight, I can't blame them. What do you say to someone who's just lost their sister? But while I was in the thick of it, their distance made me feel even more isolated. It felt like no one understood how I was feeling.

However, there was only one thing deeper than my pain and despair, and that was the love I have for my sister. For every time

I felt tempted to shut myself away in my room and just hate on the world and everyone in it, I'd see my sister's smile and immediately feel her love of life come over me. I'd feel guilty for wasting my life, when every day I get to be on this Earth is another day she doesn't. If I let myself die away with her, then her life was completely in vain.

It was this realization that gave me the push I needed to take that first step out of victimhood—the state of feeling completely helpless, like I had no control over my life or choice over how I experienced this terrible loss. I instead decided to do small things each day that would not necessarily take away my pain, but help me find just enough strength to cope with it. I would go down to the beach to watch sunrises. Get a morning coffee. Go to the gym to get a light sweat on. Write in my journal and cry on the balcony with a friend.

And while all of these things helped the grief from completely absorbing me, there was one pivotal moment that really began to reset the rest of my journey. I was lying on my bed, feeling numb and alone, when I grabbed my phone and decided to scroll through Pinterest. Before Nicole died, my Pinterest boards were filled with cute outfits or the latest fitness routine. But since her passing, I'd started pinning motivational quotes. Cheesy, I know. And I did come across the whole cliche "Believe in your dreams" type thing. They weren't so helpful. When it hurt sometimes even to breathe because the grief was so sharp in my chest, getting pep talked on my dreams wasn't helpful. But then I came across one quote that really caught me off guard. It said, "Everything can be taken from a man but one thing: the last of the human freedoms—to choose one's attitude in any given set of circumstances."

Now at first, I thought, *"Who does this guy think he is? Seriously, buddy—my sister has just been killed. I am living a nightmare right now. What do you mean I can just choose my attitude? You have no idea what you're talking about.*" But the quote intrigued me enough to want to look up the person who said it. I found the name: Viktor Frankl. And within moments I discovered just how wrong my first impressions were.

Viktor Frankl was a Holocaust survivor and one of the best Jewish psychiatrists in Austria in the 1930s. He was even working to help local high schools reduce teen suicide and depression during World War II. Then, in 1942, Frankl and his family were ordered to concentration camps by the Nazis. For three years, he was starved and enslaved as millions of innocent people around him were tortured and murdered in the horrific gas chambers, including Frankl's father, mother, brother, and even, eventually, his beautiful wife. Yet rather than becoming bitter, Frankl moved to the United States and spent his life after the war as a dedicated professor, doing all he could to teach others everything he learned about finding meaning and strength during life's worst moments.

And though his circumstances were extreme, interestingly, Frankl wasn't an outlier. In 2019, I had the honor of meeting Holocaust survivor, Eddie Jaku. There were 11,000 inmates at the first concentration camp Eddie was sent to. Over the course of the next few months, 9,000 of them would be murdered. Yet Eddie left this world in 2021 at 101 years old, proclaiming he was the "happiest man on Earth." Being in his presence, I could feel he genuinely radiated all of that warmth, that love and that positivity. His smile could light up a room. When I heard Eddie speak that day, he said "There is no revenge; living is revenge." He wanted to be a living example of everything Hitler wasn't.

As I was sitting there at my laptop, reading these heartbreaking yet inspiring stories, I just kept asking myself: "How? How could they possibly get through all of that?" My mind was blown. Yes, my heart was broken. But it was broken in an air-conditioned home with a fridge full of food and loving parents I could hug at any minute. I could not fathom how someone could possibly heal from such trauma as Viktor Frankl's and Eddie Jaku's. How don't you become bitter? How don't you give up hope? Why does adversity make some people bitter, while others seem to use it to become better? What are the things resilient people do differently?

I've made it my mission the last ten years to find an answer to this, a real, practical answer that I could use to build my own resilience. I wrote this book to help you do the same. Because there's one thing that each and every one of us have in common with Eddie Jaku, with Viktor Frankl, and with every other living and breathing example out there who proves that hardship does not have to harden you: *we are all human.* We all hold the same capacity to be resilient and learn the skills we need to rebuild from the moments in life that break us. And given you're human, it means you too can practice these tools and grow the resilience to become more adaptable to change—even the worst kind.

It all starts with one key insight that I grew up my whole life completely unaware of. If I'd known it earlier, I think it would've saved me many endless days of anxiety and meltdowns as I tried to figure out how to "adult" in this unpredictable world. The spark of this discovery began with Frankl's quote that I just shared with you, followed by another which made me rethink the helplessness that my sister's death had me spiraling into: "Between stimulus and response there is a space. And in that space lies our freedom and power to choose our responses. In our response lies our growth and our freedom."

> *"Between stimulus and response there is a space. And in that space lies our freedom and power to choose our responses. In our response lies our growth and our freedom."*
>
> *—Viktor Frankl, 1946*

The reason this quote hit home for me is because I began to realize that resilience is so much more than just positive thinking or saying happy mantras to yourself; resilience is about staying in control of what I like to call your "response-ability"—your ability to choose how you feel and how you respond to anything that happens to you. Through triumphant stories such as Frankl's, I realized that once you learn how to take back power over your response, you get back the power to change what comes next and who *you* become from any circumstance you're hit with in life. This skill of response-ability puts you back in the driver's seat of your life. You can't directly control the bends and turns of some of the roads, but you are the one navigating which detours and roads you'll choose to take. While some people may be subconsciously choosing the road to further struggle and misery by reacting to life on autopilot, this book is here to help you intentionally respond to life from a place of purpose and clarity. It's here to help you no longer feel victimized by the world so you can create something meaningful from whatever circumstances it gives you.

In fact, did you ever play the game as a kid where your friend says one word in a sentence, and then you say the next, and you go back and forth saying one word at a time, until you end up crafting a story together? You never knew what your friend might say next, but then you'd always get a choice over what you say back to them. That's how it can be with life: the world—or your friend, in the game—gives you a situation, a person, a circumstance, and then you always get a say in what comes next. And just like the game you'd play as a kid, you can't control every single detail of your life story, but the character of who you are and the overall direction that the journey takes you is always your choice. Like that friend who would sometimes throw in ridiculously random words into the game, life is going to throw you curveballs. Resilience will help you throw one right back at it by getting courageous and creative in your own meaningful way. My life changed forever when I realized I was not completely in control of the world, but I'm not completely helpless over it either. Because I am not at the mercy of what happens to me, simply my response to it. Living in the power of your response is where your greatest ability to be resilient lies.

Living in the power of your response is where your greatest ability to be resilient lies.

However, I know that *saying* you have control over how you respond to things, and actually *being* in control of your response are two very different things. In fact, sometimes it doesn't feel like how we're reacting to something is our choice at all. It feels like it's being caused by something that's way out of our control. All I ask is that you keep your mind *open* to the possibility that it is true, and why it is actually the best possible news I could have for you.

When we believe that our circumstances—what's happening in our life at any given moment—is the cause of how we're feeling or acting, we can fall into the resilience-sucking behaviors—blaming, shaming, resisting, and escaping—that only make our life harder. We can also get caught up in what I call "hamster wheel mode," where we go into a frenzied spiral of trying to control or change our circumstances or other people in order to try and feel better. For example, say you quit your job to get away from your annoying boss, changed majors at college to feel less restless, or lost ten pounds to feel more confident about your body. Sometimes changing the circumstance helps us feel better. The only issue is that the relief is typically temporary and conditional, because we're not really getting to the root cause of what's *really* making us feel that way. And then of course sometimes, as in the case of my sister's death and many other situations, controlling the situation is not even possible. No amount of wishing, praying, crying, or begging can undo or change the reality of many circumstances. So going into control mode leaves us feeling pretty helpless when we realize that we often can't really control much at all in certain situations.

I think that is what haunted me the most about my sister's death: it was so permanent. There was no countdown I could hold on to or bridge I could build to see her again. Maybe you're feeling or have felt a similar way, where you're having to come to terms with a permanent situation that feels so painful and scary that you think you're going to spend the rest of your life drowning in the emotions of it. If this is you, I see you, I hear you, I feel you. And I promise you, even if the circumstance you've been hit with is forever, how you're feeling about it right now doesn't have to be forever.

The first step we need to take toward finding relief is to let go of trying to control the external world. We only have so much energy in a day, and if we're spending time constantly trying to control things to be how we want them to be, we make ourselves crazy because it's an impossible task. Every day we're going to end up in situations that we didn't choose ourselves. So rather than go into obsessive control, blame, or avoidance mode, there is another choice that takes you from feeling victimized by your circumstances to becoming the creator of what comes next: growing your response-ability skills.

In Part 2 of the book, I'll walk you through each step of developing resilience and honing your response-ability skills so that you can begin to take back control over how any circumstance impacts you and your life. And that's what we really crave the most: a sense of control and purpose in our lives. Without a sense of autonomy or meaning in what we're going through, it's hard to find a reason to keep going through the days that feel too much to bear.

Your experiences in life do not have to be in vain. When we take responsibility for our response, we are not just puppets in a random sideshow but the directors of a movie that is our life.

Living life as a response-able adult isn't always easy, but it is always possible, and just like any other skill, it's something you get better at with practice. The good news is life gives us plenty of opportunities to practice it. Any time things go haywire, it's an opportunity for you to practice the tools I'm about to teach you so you can grow your resilience that inch more.

The most important thing to keep in mind when you're learning these skills is to channel your inner 1 year old: when you were learning how to walk, you fell down on average thirty-eight times a day. Thirty-eight times a day you'd give walking a really good go, only to end up on your backside or on your face. However, it's not like on the seventh attempt on the third day of practicing walking, you were like "Nope, that's it. I can't do it. Walking just isn't for me!" No, instead you picked yourself back up and kept trying, knowing eventually you'd get the hang of it. I need you to have the same mentality with yourself now. Let yourself be a work in progress as you learn these resilience skills and tools. Some days you'll use them to their fullest capacity and really stay in charge of your response to your cranky coworker or news that your husband's job is going to require him to stay overseas another month. Other days, you might lose your cool and let your emotions make you react in a way that you later regret. That'll happen sometimes. It still happens for me. Not because I'm not resilient, but because I'm human. And so are you.

Allow space for your humanness along this journey. Remember, resilience doesn't mean never falling down, it means getting back up every time you do. Just like you did when you were a baby and can still do now. And in the next chapters I'm going to teach you the 3 Rs to help you find your feet again, even on shaky ground.

To finish this chapter, I encourage you to step back into the role of curious observer and answer these questions in your journal or phone notes.

1. Think about how you reacted to difficult situation lately. It could be minor or major. Did you react in alignment with who you want to be as a person? Why or why not?

2. Think about a situation where you didn't react the way you wanted. How do you desire to ideally respond instead?

3. What do you think needs to change in order for you to respond in this desired way?

4. Write down the name of someone in your life that you look up to for their own resilience and ability to respond to things with intention. What advice do you think they would give you to help you better respond to the difficult situation you're struggling with?

PART 2

Recognize Your Thoughts

4

Your Thoughts Are Not Facts

I was hiking in the Daintree Rainforest in Northern Queensland, Australia, soaking up the awe-inspiring beauty of the ancient trees that were towering over me in all directions. Moss-green ferns twisted and turned their way up the 100 million-year-old trees that were as rugged as they were magnificent. Some blue-patterned butterflies fluttered past my shoulder as I took in the peaceful sound of trickling water from a nearby creek and the croaking of the frogs that had made it their home. Suddenly, I saw a snake on the path in front of me. Given the humidity and damp climate, it's not unusual for snakes to be seen there. However, I have zero bravery when it comes to snakes—or any reptile, really. So imagine the highest pitch squeal known to mankind: that was me in the middle of this majestic rainforest (I'd like to apologize to all the wildlife I disturbed who were sleeping that day). The most amusing part was, after I'd done my big song and dance and sprinted down the path faster than you can say "drama queen," my friend shouted out, "Hey, chill! That was just a stick."

This story is an accurate (and somewhat comical) example of the first "R" in becoming more response-able. No, it doesn't involve sticks or snakes, but it does focus on doing what I absolutely did not do in that situation: **recognize** that the stick was not a snake.

The first "R" to building resilience is to **recognize** what we're *thinking* about a situation and what we're making it mean in our mind. In the forest, there was no real snake on the path in front of me, but because my brain perceived it as one, I reacted as if it were. My

We are never completely helpless over how we react to circumstances or the impact that they have over our lives.

heart was thumping in my chest, and I was breathing heavily; the fear was real, but the danger was not. Meanwhile, my friend was as cool as a cucumber. Her reaction was so different because her brain interpreted it as just a stick. It's a simple story with a powerful message as to why we are never completely helpless over how we react to circumstances or the impact that they have over our lives. It all begins and ends in our own mind.

If you are having resistance to the idea that it's not really our circumstances but our *thoughts* that the cause of our feelings, it's totally understandable. I used to feel the same. But think about it this way: if other people or our circumstances really have full control over how we feel and react, then we'd all feel and react to the same circumstance in the exact same way. But, in fact, people react differently to the same situation. For example, missing out on a promotion may spiral one person into a puddle of tears and despair, while another person may be straight back to their laptop to keep chipping away at earning the boss's attention. Having to move out of an apartment because of a rent hike may cause one person to post a Facebook status ranting about her landlord, while another may immediately begin the hunt to find a more affordable housing option. The global pandemic was a worldwide example of just how many different ways we can all react to being put on lockdown and quarantined. Some people literally started fist fighting over toilet paper, while others relished the opportunity to quit their stifling job and start their own Etsy store like they always wanted. It really is fascinating to *recognize* that every minute of every day, we see so many different emotional reactions to circumstances. This is because it really does come down to which of our thoughts we believe and the way we interpret the situation—not the situation itself.

We are never, ever completely helpless when it comes to working through our emotions or overcoming the hardships in our lives, because our thoughts are not set in stone in our brain. They are the single factor in any situation that is optional, flexible, and within our power to change. And most importantly, they are not facts.

The first key to practicing resilience lies in quitting trying to control the *external* world and instead focusing on controlling our *internal* world. Naturally, we tend to want to do the opposite: change our circumstances to try to feel better. Keep begging your ex to take you back so you don't feel so lonely. Or get that PhD like your father always wanted you to so you can finally feel like you're good enough. And look, sometimes changing something in your life does work to help you feel better, like leaving an unfulfilling marriage, reporting a coworker who has made inappropriate remarks, or setting boundaries with your mother.

Often though, you will find changing your circumstances to be only a temporary solution—like a Band-Aid over a wound that really needs some antibiotics to heal. You get the PhD, and you feel a sense of accomplishment for a few weeks before you start struggling with imposter syndrome. You find a new job to get away from annoying colleagues only to find that yet another obnoxiously loud coworker is down the hall from you. That is because, wherever you go, your brain comes with you. So solving for things at a mindset level is how you create lasting change in your life that isn't dependent on circumstances. It's also what helps you change your circumstances to be more in alignment with your goals and values so you're able to create a greater sense of purpose and fulfilment in your life.

The other problem with trying to control or avoid circumstances in order to feel better is that sometimes, it's simply impossible. Every single day, you will be confronted with circumstances you cannot control or change. And if trying to control them is your only option, you're on a spaceship to the planet of Spiraling Out of Control. When we're living life in this reactive way, we're living from a place that psychologists call "external locus of control." Developed by American psychologist Julia Rotter, this is the belief that life is happening *to* us and that our circumstances are to blame for why our lives are the way they are. External locus of control sounds like, "we could've landed that client if my coworker stopped slacking off" or "my ex-boyfriend totally shattered my self-worth." You give the ownership of your life to your external circumstances or people, which is a very disempowering way to live and makes it difficult to be resilient. That's why I've found true resilience comes from building up what Rotter calls your *"internal locus of control"* by learning how to better manage the world that lives between your ears: your own mind. This begins with the step of recognizing the thoughts that are running through it and really owning that they are just thoughts.

This skillset takes practice. It is like learning a whole new way of being. Because our thoughts are so fast and automatic, we tend to believe and react to them as if they're the *actual* truth and a factual circumstance that we're dealing with. These thoughts can look something like, "My boss is out to get me!," or "No one will ever love me," or "I'm falling behind in my career." We state these things so matter-of-factly and often do what psychologist Steven C. Hayes calls *fusing* with the thought, where we almost "become" the thought and spiral into more thoughts just like it. Thought spirals are normal; the average human has over 6,000 thoughts per day, so trying to control and change every single one would send you into a frenzy more disorienting than the spinning teacup ride at Disneyland. My strategy to resilience isn't trying to control all of your thinking (because that's not even possible), it is about controlling your *response* to your thoughts.

Rather than immediately believing and reacting to every single thought as if it's fact, the first step to practice in the "R" of recognizing is to step back and see that your thinking is really causing your emotional reaction and seeing those thoughts for what they really are: language, images, and words running through your mind that only you are experiencing.

You can practice this step of recognizing your thoughts by separating out the facts in your own mind as if you're a lawyer preparing to present the facts of your case in court. Remove any sort of subjectivity, opinion, or interpretation. Because thoughts are sneaky, they're very good at dressing up as facts. Everything left over once you pull out the facts are your own thoughts and stories about the situation. When you take the time to separate out the facts of what's happening versus your own thoughts, you'll see things as they are and understand how your thoughts cause your emotional reaction— not your circumstances.

Here's a story that might help illustrate what I mean. One of my coaching clients in Alaska told me the other day that it was so warm outside she was going to go for a swim at the lake. It was fifty-seven degrees Fahrenheit. Meanwhile, in Australia, it was the same temperature, and my friend was complaining that it was too cold to wear shorts that day. Both believed they were just observing the world for what it is: it *is* warm or it *is* cold today. But what temperatures are considered hot or cold is actually a subjective choice. Not a fact. The fact was it was fifty-seven degrees. Then they attached their own preference to it and judged it as hot or cold. This is a great example of just how easy it is to assume our thoughts are facts.

Let's look at an example that's more related to building resilience. Imagine you got a flat tire on the way home from the gym, and instantly you're frustrated that you're always so unlucky. It's tempting to then spiral into anger and kick the tire for ruining your night. But if you take a minute to pull this situation apart, you can see that your flat tire isn't really what's making you frustrated. I mean, the flat tire is just sitting there; it can't jump up and implant the feeling of frustration in you. What's really causing your frustration is the thought that "you're always unlucky." When you believe that thought, of course you're going to feel frustrated. But that is just a *thought*—just an idea your brain is offering up about one possible perspective of what's happening here. The only real fact that's happened here is you have a flat tire. The rest is a made-up reality in your own mind that's causing how you feel in that moment.

Let me be clear, the end game of recognizing your thoughts isn't to strip life of all of its meaning and tell you to only think in facts. I love the capacity we have as humans to bring meaning to all different situations. It's what makes our life experience and cultures so rich. I mean, think of how differently countries around the world celebrate different traditions based on their beliefs and perspectives on life. Even death is interpreted so differently, with some cultures seeing it as a reason to celebrate and be joyous, while others mourn and lament. Our brain's capacity to add meaning and stories to our circumstances is what makes our life so fulfilling, and at times, so hard and painful. Especially if the meaning or stories we're telling ourselves don't serve us. But we can't change what we're not aware of; that's why this step of *recognizing* our thoughts rather than just reacting to them, is so important. Let's give it a try now with a couple of prompts, and then we'll expand more on it in Chapter 6.

Take out a piece of paper or a notebook or scan the QR code to get access to a worksheet designed for this exercise. Brain dump everything you're thinking and feeling about a situation you're currently struggling with: What happened? How are you feeling about it and why?

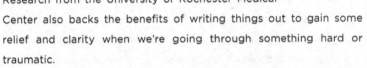

Don't worry about editing yourself here, just let it *all* out like you're ranting to a friend. In fact, I love the relief writing out my own thoughts and feelings brings me, so it's not just spiraling around my own head. Research from the University of Rochester Medical Center also backs the benefits of writing things out to gain some relief and clarity when we're going through something hard or traumatic.

Then, to prevent spiraling further into these thoughts, read over what you wrote. Underneath, write out the neutral facts of what's really going on. Then, list the main thoughts that are causing your feelings about the situation. Here's an example.

> **Brain Dump:** *My boss laughed at my idea in front of the entire meeting and now everyone thinks I'm completely incompetent. There goes my chance of a promotion. I'm feeling so ashamed right now.*
>
> **Fact:** Boss laughed at idea I suggested
>
> **Thought:** "Everyone thinks I'm completely incompetent, so there goes my chance of a promotion."
>
> **Feeling:** Ashamed

Now that we've separated out the facts versus the thoughts, you can recognize the thoughts that are really causing how you feel.

A powerful way to reinforce this to yourself—that it's really your thoughts that are impacting you the most—is to try this little exercise:

1. Write how you're feeling about what's happening and why
2. Cross out that sentence
3. Rewrite that sentence, inserting the words *"because I'm thinking the thought"* right before the thought you recognize is upsetting you the most. Identifying your thoughts as thoughts helps you step back and create space from your thinking rather than spiraling further into it as if it's something happening *to* you that you can't control.

RECOGNIZE:

~~I'm feeling ashamed, because everyone thinks I'm incompetent, so there goes my chance of promotion.~~

I'm feeling ashamed *because I'm thinking the thought* that everyone thinks I'm incompetent so there goes my chance of promotion.

Here's another example:

Brain Dump: *I'm so frustrated that another two year relationship ended in a break up. It was all a waste.*
Fact: My relationship ended after two years
Thought: "It was all a waste."
Feeling: Frustrated

RECOGNIZE:

~~I'm feeling frustrated because my two year relationship was all a waste.~~

I'm feeling frustrated *because I'm thinking the thought* that my two year relationship was all a waste.

Having awareness of your own thoughts changes everything. This was a real moment of growth for me when I realized this about my sister's death. I didn't want to feel so much anger and resentment at the world for what happened. I wanted to live life to the fullest again in her honor. I realized the solution to that wasn't to turn back time and stop her death from ever happening (as much as I wish I could); I instead needed to find a way to shift my focus on the whole event. Because naturally I was spinning in thoughts like, "This is so unfair. That driver has ruined my family's life. I'll never be happy again without my sister." But taking my power back began by recognizing these are just thoughts about what happened, not facts. The only fact is that my sister died. Everything else is my story and interpretation of it all.

Stepping back and pulling out your thoughts about a situation is what takes you out of victimhood and connects you back with your own internal locus of control: your ability to choose your response based on your perspective. Because if I believed my painful story about my sister's death as fact, that the driver did ruin my family's life, I would have given him all of the control over how her death impacts me and kept myself stuck in the bitterness of it all. But by being able to see that circumstances within themselves have no meaning—they're just existing and happening in the world like the temperature outside or the weather, we can stop feeling victimized by the circumstances of our lives.

In fact, there is a quote from Shakespeare's *Hamlet* after his father had been killed and he felt imprisoned in Denmark, that gives me a way to steady myself when I feel the urge to panic about something that's happening in my life as if it's inherently bad. It helps slow me down a little and redirect my focus to be more mindful of my thoughts: "Nothing is either good or bad, but thinking makes it so."

This quote is powerful to help us remember to step back and notice where our mind is adding meaning, judgment, or interpretation to what is factually happening. Recognizing your thoughts like this might not instantly make you feel better, but it does give you back the thing you're craving the most, a sense of control and freedom of choice. Just like Viktor Frankl said: "Between stimulus and response there is a space. And in that space lies our freedom and power to choose our responses." Our minds are something we *can* change, and building our ability to be more psychologically flexible and adaptive is what I'll teach you in the future Rs.

In Chapter 5, you'll learn about a few things that really helped me overcome all the obstacles that got in the way of me trying to change my thinking initially. Given you're human, you're likely going to run into these obstacles, too. Our human brains are amazing and also complicated. They do have the capacity to change and learn new patterns of thinking, but it's not as simple as flipping a switch. So if you've ever tried to change your thoughts before but felt like you were stuck with the same damn ones as the day before, this next chapter will help you understand more about why and what you can do to finally change your mindset.

5

Brain Biases to Look Out For

Now that you understand how most of our stress and reactions in life come down to what we *think* about our circumstances, it's time to talk about how our brain has certain built-in ways of functioning that make it challenging to instantly change our thoughts and behaviors. Because it's one thing to intellectually understand that thoughts create feelings, so you can change your thinking in order to be more resilient, but actually putting it into practice can be tough. Before I understood this, I had so much judgment of my own thoughts and negativity. I'd see the "Just believe in yourself!" and "Be positive!" quotes online, but all of that felt so beyond reach when every day, all day long, my brain would be throwing negativity at me like confetti. I felt stuck. It took learning everything about how my brain is wired to get unstuck, which is why I made sure it's a part of this book for you, too.

Contrary to what I once thought, looping over the past or dwelling on your losses isn't a sign that you're just a "negative thinker" or that you're stuck being an anxious overthinker forever. What's beneath a lot of these mental habits aren't flaws to be ashamed of, but normal features of the human brain to be understood. Once you understand that it's natural for your brain to do certain things, you can gain so much more traction over managing your mind because you can anticipate how your brain will likely react automatically to certain situations and then how you want to respond to it from there. These are the mental health lessons I wish I had learned at school to better understand what it means to have a human brain and not think, "There's something wrong with me," when I couldn't instantly think positively, even when I could see the benefit of it.

So now that you know the purpose of this chapter, let's dive into what these main brain biases are and how to better spot them before you let them hijack your reactions. We're going to briefly explore the brain's motivational triad and prefrontal cortex, as well as *negativity bias* and *confirmation bias*. Think of this chapter like the "troubleshooting" chapter you can refer back to any time you feel like you're in a rut, and your brain keeps getting the better of you.

Motivational Triad

I'd be a rich lady if I got a dollar every time someone says, "I try to change my mindset or think differently, but it just feels weird and hard." They're right; it absolutely does. And I know that can be defeating. However, the reason your brain tries to prevent you from changing your mindset isn't because it wants to make your life miserable and cause you to suffer; in fact, it's the opposite. Your brain loves you so much that its number-one mission is to keep you safe and alive. It wants to protect you above all costs, so it resists change.

This basic survival function is what psychologists call the motivational triad and is part of what's kept our human species going for hundreds of thousands of years. Because of the motivational triad, our brain is always motivated to do three basic functions: seek pleasure and comfort, avoid pain and discomfort, and exert as little energy as possible. This all makes sense from a purely survival standpoint during evolution; when our great great uncle x 10,000 was living in a cave, it made sense not to seek out dangers like fires on the horizon or new trails in the forest that could be filled with venomous snakes, and it was best to stay in the cave and conserve energy. Because who knows, you might need to fight a tiger later, so it's best we stay safe and keep chewing on some berries, just in case! The motivational triad was critical to helping humans survive back in hunter-gatherer days. However, in today's society, doing only what's easy and avoiding anything difficult is literally the opposite of what you need to do to achieve any goal that we have—like changing our mindset.

Because the human brain wants to be comfortable, avoid pain, and conserve energy, it also hates change—period. It loves certainty and equilibrium and for things to remain as they are, because that way it can best predict what may happen next so it can keep you safe. This means your brain likes to keep thinking the same thoughts and believing the same beliefs it already has, because those neural pathways are well ingrained in your subconscious and easy for your brain to do with ease and speed. They are like superhighways that your brain travels on anytime you're in a familiar situation. In fact, your brain is a pattern-making machine—once we repeat something over and over on a regular basis, like checking our blind spot driving, tying our shoelaces, or chewing our nails, it takes those memorized neural pathways and puts it in our subconscious mind so it all happens on autopilot. This is what makes a habit; it's something you do so automatically that you barely even notice you're doing it half the time. Just like we have

Just like we have physical habits with our behavior and actions, we have thinking habits within our own mind.

physical habits with our behavior and actions, we have thinking habits within our own mind.

For example, whenever you're meeting with your bosses and you start feeling anxious, that feeling hasn't just "come over you" because you're near your bosses. It's because every time you're around your managers, you've repeated over and over thoughts like, "I'm going to say the wrong thing," or "I don't have any good ideas," so that before you're even aware of it, your subconscious mind is firing these thoughts. Upon reflection, you can intellectually see that perhaps thinking positive thoughts like, "I have value to contribute to the conversation" and "I belong in this room" would help you feel a lot less anxious about the meeting. However, when you tell yourself these thoughts, your brain rejects them instantly and keeps spewing the negative thoughts at you. It's tempting to think that those negative thoughts really must be true, that your brain won't believe the new thoughts because the old ones are the "true" ones. But that's not the case. The reason your brain holds on to its old pattern of thinking is because it's the familiar one that's easiest to think.

I like to nickname the motivational triad "the toddler in our brain," because it behaves a lot like one. It throws a tantrum of resistance when we change our routine or try to shift our mindset. It prefers to take lots of naps, have fun stuff *now*, and avoid anything it doesn't feel like doing. It means well, but it usually ends up causing us more struggle when we let it call the shots. Trying to think differently than your current pattern of thinking is like asking your brain "Hey, instead of speeding along this smooth highway in a Ferrari, let's forge a new trail by foot through the thick, dense forest of the Amazon." Since that's going to take way more effort, the brain resists thinking these new thoughts. So please don't judge yourself when you find your brain keeps spinning in old thoughts and struggles to instantly believe new ones. That doesn't make you negative or stuck or hopeless; it makes you human.

Now, the good news is just because changing our thinking can be hard and full of effort, it's definitely not impossible, thanks to our prefrontal cortex that sits on top of our "toddler brain." The prefrontal cortex is the part of our brain where we have the ability to think about what we think about and decide on purpose where we direct our attention. It's where we memorize new information, plan, set goals, and consciously make decisions about what we want most, not just how we feel in the moment or what our motivational triad naturally defaults to. This part of the brain that gives us the power of choice is the greatest gift that we have as humans.

Remember Viktor Frankl's quote about the space between stimulus and response? I believe that space he was talking about is our prefrontal cortex. That part of our brain might not give us direct control over how we feel in that moment, but it does give us power back over our actions. It allows us to become aware of our thoughts without becoming them or acting them out on impulse. It helps us create more space between what we think and what we do.

So if the primitive motivational triad in our brain is like a toddler, think of our prefrontal cortex as the "adult" in our brain. We can't get rid of the toddler; it's a built-in part of being human. But we can learn how to manage the toddler using our "parent" prefrontal cortex, which can override some of the natural yet unhelpful motivational instincts that keep us stuck repeating old habits.

Even though this takes time and persistence, the effort to change your thoughts and pattern of thinking is never in vain. Scientists have discovered in recent decades that we can change and rewire our brain with deliberate practice and repetition—they call it *neuroplasticity*. This means that the millions of neural pathways in our brain are malleable, like plastic. Once we consciously repeat a particular thought or behavior over and over again, the neural pathways of that thought or action cause stronger and deeper grooves in our brain.

Psychologists often use the analogy of a skier riding down the edge of a mountain through snow. The first time the skier goes down, they have to forge a shallow path through the snow that may be tough to ride through at first. But if that skier follows that same path twenty times over, the groove of that path will get deeper and deeper every time, making it easier and easier for that skier to ride down. The same thing happens in our brains when we consciously repeat a thought or action. Or as neuropsychologist Donald Hebb once said, "Neurons that fire together, wire together."

So never lose hope in your ability to change your habits of thinking; if you put effort into repeating new thoughts often enough, your brain will begin to adapt to thinking them more often on autopilot and travel the pathway of your old thoughts less. You *can* change your brain, it just won't happen by chance. But it will happen by conscious choice and practice to override the "motivational triad" instincts of your brain to conserve energy and stick to what it knows. Those instincts once helped keep us alive, but now they're keeping us from truly living our best lives. We need to evolve past the survival mechanisms that got us here and learn how to better engage our purposeful brain to respond to challenges in a way that creates more of the change we want in our lives. This means we also need to get a handle over one of the biggest biases in our brain that can cause havoc for us: the negativity bias.

Negativity Bias

The partner bias to the motivational triad is negativity bias. As often as you may see "Be happy and live in the moment" messages plastered all over social media, our brain is designed to do anything but. Our brains have not evolved to make us happy and think positive naturally. If they were, our species might not still be here. I mean, can you imagine your great grandma x 1,000 saying, "Oh don't worry Ted, that big bear over there probably loves a good cuddle!" or "Yes! Let's build our hut right on the edge of that cliff—we'll be all right!"? Yeah, optimistic thinking wouldn't have likely ended well for our ancestors.

Instead, our brains learned early on that it's always best to assume that a stick on the path is a snake and err on the side of caution than to hope it's just a stick and learn the hard (and deadly!) way that it was a snake. In fact, as we heard in my Daintree story in the beginning of Chapter 4, that's exactly what my brain did. And as ridiculous as I looked and sounded in my reaction, it actually wasn't me being silly—it was me being human. Our brains are designed to scan and look for potential threats, dangers, and signs that things have or could go wrong. In fact, neuroscientist and psychologist Rick Hanson explained that positive information and experiences are like Teflon to our brain—it tends to slide right off and not be something your brain gives much weight to because things like enjoying a pretty sunset or a good laugh with your friend are not as important to your survival. Potentially negative information, on the other hand, like your colleague sniggering at your suggestion in the team meeting or the doctor warning that you have a high risk of developing skin cancer, tends to stick like Velcro because our brains have learned that that information is more important to keep you safe and alive.

In today's society where we have plenty of access to food, water and safety, our brain dwelling over things like a sniggering colleague is not at all vital to your survival. We no longer depend on a tribe to live, so you don't need every single person in your town or workplace or social media following to like you. However, your brain perceives any sign of discomfort—whether it's physical, psychological or emotional—all at the same level of danger. It thinks that the racing heart and sweaty palms that you get as you stand up to deliver your annual presentation to the entire workplace is as deadly as a Bengal tiger chasing you. So the fact your brain interpreted that snickering colleague as a threat makes sense, given its job is to sense any potential misfortune and ring the alarm when it does.

However, just like the fire alarm in your home, your brain doesn't always get it right. Sometimes it's just a candle you blew out letting off some smoke and not your actual house on fire. But our primitive brain doesn't know this. Its job is to jump to the worst case scenario to protect us, and then it's our job as humans to use the prefrontal cortex to really assess the situation and bring it back to a more accurate, balanced view of reality.

It's helpful to be aware of the negativity bias in your brain, because whenever anything happens that is uncertain or unexpected, you can now know ahead of time that your brain is instinctively likely to dwell on the negative and interpret things as threats or harmful. The best term I've heard for these types of thoughts was coined by psychologist Dr. Daniel Amen: ANTs or Automatic Negative Thoughts. When you're about to walk up to introduce yourself to your date, and you hear that sneaky voice say, "He already doesn't like you; look at how he's looking at you!", you can remember it's just your brain being like an overprotective father, trying to save you from potential harm and not something to spiral into instantly as if it's truth.

We all have ANTs, and we can't stop them from coming. And sometimes we don't want them to, especially if it helps us take action against something dangerous, like wearing sunscreen to reduce your risk of developing skin cancer. But most of the time these ANTs are firing up unnecessarily in situations where there really is no physical danger present, just a struggle or a challenge that the brain is jumping to negative conclusions about. It's impossible to control every single thought in our brain, but what we *do* have control over is changing our response to our automatic thoughts, thanks to our prefrontal cortex and the neuroplasticity of our brain.

Confirmation Bias

I find confirmation bias fascinating. Once you become aware of it, you can see just how much it's controlling your subconscious and keeping you stuck in your current cycle of beliefs. Here's a scenario that most of us have experienced in life that shows how confirmation bias works. Say you're convinced barbeque sauce isn't in your pantry, so you ask, and your partner tells you to look harder. You give the pantry another look, but you swear you can't see in there. You're starting to get frustrated by this point, so your partner comes into the kitchen to look for it, and bam! They find your beloved barbeque sauce in your pantry in two seconds, and you're thinking "How did I not see that?!"

No, you're not blind or crazy. It's because you believed the sauce wasn't there, and your subconscious mind filtered what you were seeing in front of you to prove that belief true. Your partner, on the other hand, irrefutably knew they put it in in the pantry the night before and had full belief that they would find it there—and so their eyes filtered what they were seeing differently to prove that true and help them see the sauce. You'll also notice it with things like when you decide you want to rent a house downtown, and you start noticing "for rent" signs on houses that had been there for weeks but you had previously never paid attention to. As once said by the

French philosopher Henri Bergson, "The eye sees what the mind looks for."

Once your brain believes something is true or relevant, it becomes like a used car salesperson, justifying its perspective and finding evidence for its beliefs. Not because it actually believes that specific thought is a fact; it's just doing what it's designed to do—looking for evidence in the world that reinforces its current thoughts, while dismissing evidence that contradicts them or could prove them wrong. One way confirmation bias is actually helpful is that it stops our brain from getting overwhelmed by trying to take in all the million sensory data points happening in the world at once. Your brain needs to figure out what's worth focusing on and what's not, so it developed a Reticular Activation System (RAS). The RAS filters anything that enters your brain and only lets in the data points that align with what you already believe to be true, important, or relevant. And that is why our brain then dismisses any evidence that might disprove its point of view and actively seeks out proof for why its current beliefs are true.

Here's an example of how this works. If you believe the thought, "I'm never going to get over the breakup with my ex," your brain is subconsciously scanning throughout your day for evidence why that's true. The evidence could be that you feel a pang in your heart when you see your ex's Instagram account, or you might look around and hope you'll run into your ex in the food court near work. Your brain will take these as examples that your assumption was right, and then you'll start feeling even worse about yourself and dig further into that belief. In the meantime, it'll ignore the fact that you're still getting up and about your day without your ex being a part of it, you just got a promotion at work, and you have been invited to join friends on a trip to Cabo next month. You have plenty of evidence as to how you're starting to move forward and are doing a decent job at healing from the break up, but because your brain is running the "I'm never going to get over this" soundtrack, it doesn't filter these things into your awareness as being relevant to focus on.

Confirmation bias means we're all figuratively walking around this Earth wearing invisible glasses, and the lens through which you're seeing the world is based on what you believe about it. This is so important to be aware of, because so often people approach life from this place of "I'll believe it once I see it." They might think, "I'll believe that I'm capable at being promoted once my boss makes me the offer," or "I'll believe that I'll find an amazing life partner once I meet that person." It sounds logical until you realize that's not at all how our mind works. In fact, it's the opposite. Your brain will never really see and absorb any new beliefs or information until it believes there's a possibility it is true. So instead of approaching your life from a place of "I'll believe it once I see it," the resilience you're seeking and the results you want in your life will become so much easier to create once you flip that to "I'll begin to see it once I choose to believe it."

Just because you *have* believed something is true for your whole life doesn't mean you have to keep believing that thought. Neuroplasticity gives us the chance to change our beliefs, because they are nothing more than thoughts we've thought so often that they're ingrained into our brain on autopilot. We think we're just stating the way we are or the way the world is. But as we explored in Chapter 4, anything that's subjective is a thought, and any thought can be changed. Using your prefrontal cortex, you have the power to decide on purpose what you want to choose to believe and train your mind to believe it.

In order to train your brain, you have to start telling yourself a different story about what you believe so you start to use confirmation bias in your own favor. Maybe you're constantly thinking thoughts like, "Things never work out for me" or "My career is ruined now." It's time to change the narrative. Here's a great exercise that will help you flip the script on your confirmation bias and begin retraining your brain. This exercise gives your brain the evidence it craves in order to stop believing the negative thoughts about yourself. Once it sees that evidence, it begins to stop resisting so hard and the new thought begins to feel more and more true.

Grab a pen and paper, or the journal you've set aside to be your companion along your resilience journey, or open up the Notes app on your phone. Write at the top a belief you'd ideally like to believe but that currently feels beyond reach. Then, write down evidence as to why it's true. For example, if you want to believe life is working out in your favor, you could write down anything that proves that to be true. Perhaps your dress for the end of year work party arrived the night before and fit perfectly. Or maybe you chose the fastest moving line at the grocery store or ran into a friend you hadn't seen in a while on the subway who invited you out for drinks.

I encourage you to do this exercise every day for the next 30 days. If you're not sure where to start, use my example: "Life's working out in my favor." If that feels too hard to wrap your mind around right now, then add in the words "It's possible" to the front of the thought: "It's possible that life's working out in my favor." Adding "it's possible" to the front of the thought is a way to stop your brain from completely shutting down, as your brain can't argue with the fact there's a possibility that thought could be true and softens it a little so it's more open minded about it. You may notice that when you first introduce new beliefs to your brain, the confirmation bias may initially resist them, but don't let that resistance be the reason you quit on changing your mindset. It's a natural part of the process!

This exercise is exactly what I did after my sister died, and I was trying to keep myself out of complete victimhood, but thinking positively about things didn't feel realistic either. I began telling myself "It's possible something good could come from this." At first, I had no clue what that could even be. But the possibility of it piqued my brain's interest enough to begin to look out into the world and find examples of how that could be true and replaced my helplessness with a sense of curiosity and hope. That curiosity and hope then gave me the strength I needed to begin to take action. I looked for support groups and started speaking to other people who had lost a loved one for guidance and advice.

Many people roll their eyes when I tell them that good things can come from any situation you go through. Their confirmation bias rejects that idea, and a whole range of negative beliefs come tumbling out about how unfair life has been. Now, I get it, there's time for venting and letting out your frustration. But when you live life from that victimhood mindset, the confirmation bias in your brain is going to keep reinforcing and finding proof for those unhelpful beliefs. Remember, if you hold a negative outlook on something, it will literally keep scanning the world for that negativity, which only makes you feel worse and act in even more unhelpful ways. Nothing good is going to come from that situation if you've taken no productive action to make that happen because your beliefs were getting in the way.

The reason I was able to create my sister's charity was because I began believing that there was the possibility something good could come from her loss. Through that belief, I found the strength, hope, and creativity to make good things happen. The belief came first, not the other way around. That is why it's so important you become aware of what you currently believe and not let your confirmation bias run wild on proving true old, outdated beliefs that don't serve you.

What we've covered in this chapter is only a short introduction to all that you can learn about our incredibly intricate brains. I hope that understanding these brain biases helps you as much as it did me in getting traction to build a better mindset. Remember: Your brain resisting new thoughts initially is normal. Your brain jumping to the negatives is normal. Your brain defaulting back to old thoughts (even when you don't want to think them anymore) is normal. These are all normal features of our brain that we have to anticipate coming up along the way and not make it mean anything other than "I am human." Sometimes I even say to myself, "I see you brain, I see you wanting to overthink every possible worst case scenario that could happen now that my plane has been delayed or someone dissed my book in an Amazon review. I see you trying to protect me, but it's really not necessary right now. There's no real danger here. I am safe."

Being able to step back and recognize the biases of my brain unfolding in real time has helped me be so much less reactive and so much more response-able to the hard things in life. I let them happen without getting attached to them or getting frustrated at myself "why am I doing this again??!" I encourage you to do the same, to engage your own inner "parent" in your brain, and notice when your "toddler" is resisting a new habit or your negativity bias is going into overdrive, and without judgment or panic, step back and hold space for your humanness. We can't eject these tendencies of our brain, but we can stop letting them control our actions by taking them out of the driver's seat and putting them back where toddlers belong—in the baby seat in the back of the car. Get back in the driver's seat of your life and know that, with effort and practice, you can rewire your brain to be more resilient. In the chapters ahead, I am going to teach you the steps and strategies you need to do exactly that—to feel more in charge of your own brain and override the automatic instincts that distract us from staying in control over our own response to the unexpected things in life.

Get back in the driver's seat of your life and know that, with effort and practice, you can rewire your brain to be more resilient.

PART 3

Reflect on How Your Thoughts Impact You

6

Breaking the Cycle

Before a mechanic is able to fix a car, they have to know how the car works and how all the different parts of it come together to make the car operate. The same goes with our brain—if we want to change the way we think, we have to understand some of our brain's basic features first. That way we can learn to work with it, rather than against it. This is crucial, because at any given minute, the thoughts we're having about a situation cause how we're feeling and reacting to it. Recognizing those thoughts is the first step to gaining power back over the situation.

In this chapter, I'd like to go a step further beyond recognizing your thoughts to **reflecting** on how your thoughts impact you. This is the second "R" in the three Rs to resilience. This step is essential, because not only do our thoughts create our feelings, our thoughts and feelings actually drive all of our actions. As humans, we behave a particular way based on how we're thinking and feeling in that moment. There are simple examples of this everywhere: If we're feeling super unmotivated to finish a work project, we'll likely procrastinate. If we're feeling really excited about a date, we'll throw on some music to groove to while we get ready. If we're feeling anxious, we'll pick at our cuticles or

Our thoughts and feelings are the fuel for our actions and behavior.

fidget with our zipper. Our thoughts and feelings are the fuel for our actions and behavior. And then it's what we do (or don't do) based on how we're feeling and thinking that will create our outcome and how that situation impacts our lives.

This step of "reflecting" is powerful because as we just explored, our brains have an instinct to keep holding onto our current thoughts and justifying why they're true so it doesn't have to put effort into changing them. And sometimes, we might not want to. Sometimes what we go through is so difficult that it feels impossible to change the negative thoughts about the situation. If that's you, I want you to know I get you. I really do.

I have people I coach who say that exact thing to me all the time: "Why should I change my thoughts about this? It's not fair!" One young man I was coaching has hyperpigmentation on his face. Any attempts to open his mind to reframing this condition to cause him to feel less helpless about it was initially met with utmost resistance. "*I don't want to feel good about this. Everyone is judging me for it, and it's so hard to make friends or find a date.*"

I also coached a woman in her early 20s whose father had an affair and caused the whole family to go through a messy divorce during her final year at school. I could feel her anger at him for putting the family through that and betraying her trust so deeply. "*If my own father can do this, how can I ever trust anyone? It seems like no relationships last these days.*" For many sessions she'd spiral into this place of blame over what happened. I saw the way he'd shattered her innocence of who she thought he was and what her family was all about. Things never felt the same for her after that.

That's something I can really empathize with. When my sister died, so did the family that I once knew. Suddenly, birthdays weren't just to celebrate, but to make space for a little empty hole in our hearts knowing that Nicole wasn't there to share it with us. Christmases now meant trips to the cemetery to visit her, and speaking about Nicole often meant seeing pain in my Mum's eyes that I wish I could take away, but I couldn't. Nicole missed out on being at my twenty-first birthday, my thirtieth birthday, my graduation, my wedding, and my book launches. So many milestones, big and small, that have felt a little emptier because my sister wasn't there. And I hate that. I truly do.

Thinking positively about these moments when I miss my sister is not something I ever want to do. I don't want to feel good about the grief my family has been forced to live with. And my thoughts on her death very early on were justifiably filled with anger, fear, and pain. I was so mad at the driver for being so heartless. *"Why did you have to ride on the wrong side? Why did you never apologize to my family? I hate you for ruining my family's life."* I was also mad at the local police and their lack of respect toward my family after Nicole died. I was mad they didn't seek any justice or seem to care about how it felt to bring a loved one home from a vacation in a pine box.

I'm sure most people would understand if I had chosen to live life from that bitter perspective, as I certainly felt very justified in thinking that way. Most likely, you've gone through something unfair in life where it is reasonable for you to have bitter and angry thoughts, too. So I'm not here to judge any of your thoughts as crazy or weak or unnecessary, especially when we often have a lot of evidence that can prove how much harder your life has been since that thing happened. That's the sneaky little confirmation bias at play here!

Now, let's look at what happens when all of us from the scenarios above—my client who felt like he had a difficult time making friends because of the hyperpigmentation on his face, my client whose father had an affair, or me feeling bitterness toward my sister's death and its circumstances—recognized that we were having negative thoughts and then went a step further by reflecting on how those thoughts made them feel and behave. When I asked my client with hyperpigmentation how the thought "*I'll never make friends because of how I look*" made him feel, he admitted that he feels so insecure that be becomes more standoffish, overthinks what everyone around him could be thinking of him, less likely to start up conversation or invite someone to grab lunch with him, loses his sense of humor, stumbles when he speaks, and usually spends a lot of time in the mirror nitpicking himself apart. He said because of this he feels more isolated and like an outcast to everyone else.

And the woman whose father had an affair realized that her thought "*It seems like no relationships last these days*" had made her act more hostile and clingy. She'd been needing constant reassurance from her boyfriend and found she was quicker to get mad and accuse him of lying, which often led to them arguing and her giving him the silent treatment.

And for me, of course I was tempted to stay angry and bitter at the world for now having to live the rest of my life without my sister in it. I wanted to keep insisting that "*No! She should still be alive!*" I do still want my sister to be just a phone call away. But if I dwelled over a reality that could never be real again, I'd cement my own helplessness that made me want to shut the world out and never leave my room. It made me want to complain about everything and ruminate over all the "what ifs" and "if onlys" that kept me stuck in the past.

This is when I began to realize how helpful this step of "reflection" can be. Your thoughts may be justified, but given they influence your actions and behavior, resilience is about being mindful of their impact on your outcomes. Brooke Castillo, founder of the Life Coach School, taught me it in this very simplified way:

Step 1: You have thoughts about a particular situation.
Step 2: Those thoughts cause your feelings.

Step 3: Your feelings drive your behavior.

Step 4: Your behavior influences your outcome.

Here's a good example. You've been interviewed for a promotion at work, but it ends up going to your colleague who's been there only six months and doesn't have as many clients as you. You might be tempted to think that your boss is trying to sabotage your career. Of course, if you believe that thought, you'll feel hurt, angry and stressed. While you may feel justified in thinking this way, reflect on how you typically act around the workplace and your colleagues when you feel angry and stressed. It could mean you begin to have unhelpful behavior like complaining to colleagues, talking behind the boss's back, slacking off work ("*I mean, what's the point? I'm not going to get promoted anyway!*"), skipping meetings, or simply not producing your most creative work.

Research by Dr. Wendy Suzuki, a neuroscientist at New York University, shows that when we're spinning in negative thoughts and feelings like anger, resentment, and helplessness, our mindset narrows. It closes up, and we can't see possibilities, options, or solutions. Negative emotion shuts down our ability to problem solve, think creatively, or call upon the resources that can help us move forward, like researching other jobs or chatting with the boss about concrete goals that will get you to the promotion you want. Instead, we get caught dwelling on the problem, ruminating over it, and often lashing out at ourselves or others. Acting that way at work is a one-way ticket to sabotaging your own chances of future promotions, because you're making it harder for your boss or colleagues to like and trust you. And suddenly it feels like your colleagues are enemies, your boss is a jerk, and you're getting fewer and fewer new clients sent your way.

Although it feels like your brain is a fortune teller that predicted that your boss was out to ruin your career, it's really because you were continually thinking that way, it caused you to feel and act in ways that proved that true. That's why our thoughts begin to feel more and more real to us. Our thoughts subconsciously make us act in ways that create more evidence for them, which the confirmation bias in our brains loves.

It really is as simple as this: Life doesn't happen *to* you. Life happens. But how it impacts you is entirely up to you. It's based on your *response* to the circumstance—not the circumstance itself.

Since our thoughts dictate the way we respond to circumstances, it's important to take a beat and notice how those thoughts make you feel and behave. The most useful question to reflect on is, "Are my thoughts helpful?" A helpful thought is one that helps you take productive action or show up in a way that you're proud of. Once you're able to identify how a thought makes you feel bad and react poorly to something, it does begin to become easier to loosen your brain's grip on those thoughts and open it up to finding another perspective.

You might have heard another approach where you ask yourself, "Is that thought really true? What evidence do you have to support it? Or disprove it?" While these kinds of questions can be helpful sometimes, unless there's some obvious example of why the thought isn't really true, typically the brain's confirmation bias will miss these examples, and its resistance to changing its current beliefs usually bites back with even more reasons to reinforce the negative thought. That just leaves you caught in a mental tug of war of what's true or what's not. Because at the end of the day, what's true for you is whatever you believe to be true. So I don't think it's relevant whether a thought is "true" or not, it's about whether the thought is *helpful* or not. When you're stuck in a place of self-pity and resentment, this question will help you be more intentional and prevent unhelpful actions that could lead to more negative outcomes for you.

Remember when my client with hyperpigmentation realized that his negative thoughts made him feel more isolated and alone? This is the exact opposite of what he wants for himself. By helping him reflect on how his self-judgment about his condition and his assumption that everyone judges him for it only creates more disconnection and isolation from his colleagues, he did begin to stop justifying to me why those thoughts are so true. That was his first step toward change. He let go of what was weighing him down the most: his own thoughts about his hyperpigmentation, not the hyperpigmentation itself.

Same with my client who was trapped in a cycle of blaming her father's cheating for his mistrust in relationships. When she spiraled into her negative thoughts, she reflected on how she acted towards her current boyfriend. When she told me she was acting more hostile and clingy, you could tell it was difficult for her, because she looked at me nearly ready to get defensive. Then I gently reminded her not to judge herself, as I certainly wasn't judging her. She had good reason for her current beliefs about relationships, but were they helpful to keep holding on to? Her reflection on how those insecure thoughts made her act like the controlling and needy girlfriend she never wanted to be helped her to realize that her beliefs were driving more of a wedge into her relationship. That's the ironic thing; when we're worried about someone leaving us or being untrustworthy, we can act in ways that typically push them away and create more distance, which ultimately leads to more distrust and disconnection.

When you're able to recognize your own thoughts and reflect on how they're playing into the dynamic of your life—your actions and the outcomes they create for you—you gain back that sense of power over your life. We have the freedom to choose which thoughts to focus on and let drive our actions, and which ones to let go of, because they're simply not worth the outcome they create.

Once I recognized and reflected on how much my thoughts about how terrible my life would be without my sister made me dwell on a past I couldn't fix, causing me to stay stuck in bitterness, my life started to change. The past is over. It's gone. The only place we can live in is today, and by reflecting on how unhelpful it was to stay spinning over what I think "should" be different but don't have the ability to change, I was causing myself so much extra suffering. It's like life pushes us into a ditch, and whether we begin to climb our way out or dig ourselves further in comes down to our perspective and our response. Responding to life's challenges with negativity and blame only makes us do the latter: act in ways that digs us further into the ditch of struggle and pain.

Too many people sit back and think, "I'll let go of my bitterness at not being promoted or being diagnosed with Lyme disease once my life starts to get better," but that's not the way it works. You have to be willing to let go of the negativity and blame *first* in order to fuel the strength and determination you need to take more helpful action. Your action has to be aligned with the outcome you want, which means your thoughts and perspective have to be aligned with that outcome as well.

You can't fill up a car with soda and expect it to run well. In fact, it doesn't go anywhere at all. It's not the right fuel. Same goes with us. We can't be filled with bitterness and expect to get any momentum going forward, because it makes us want to do the opposite: ruminate, complain, hide away, and distract ourselves. Life is too short to live in a self-defeating cycle of shame and blame. It robs you of resilience and your own life experience.

Life is too short to live in a self-defeating cycle of shame and blame. It robs you of resilience and your own life experience.

So now we've gone through these examples, and you understand the power of the Reflect stage, it's time to pull out your notebook or Notes app on your phone. Let's get curious about reflecting on one of the situations you wrote about in the Recognize exercise in Chapter 4, where you separated out the facts from your thoughts and recognized which thoughts that are causing you the struggle the most. Refer back to what you wrote there. Now, I want you to answer the following three questions:

1. How do I act or behave in this situation or around this person when I believe these thoughts?
2. What outcome does this behavior create for me? (e.g. Does it typically lead to more tension or conflict in the relationship? Missing deadlines and running behind on projects? More loneliness or distance from other people in your life?)

Now that you've reflected on the outcome these thoughts ultimately create for you based on how they make you feel and behave, answer the third and most important question:

3. Are these thoughts helpful: do they help me take action toward my goals or act in a way that I'm proud of?

If your answer for this final question is "no," please don't judge yourself. The essential ingredient to the Reflect stage is to ensure you're coming at it from a place of curiosity, not criticism. Your brain is doing the best it can to make sense of the world. So don't beat yourself up for thinking any thought. Thoughts pop up automatically from our subconscious for a whole range of reasons that are sometimes unexplainable. We're not responsible for those ANTs, and they're not a moral reflection of who we are as a human. We just want to become aware of them and reflect on the impact they're having on our lives when they

drive our actions. Be curious and fascinated when you can begin to connect the dots and finally recognize why you've been caught in a cycle
of self-sabotage or struggle.

This insight is so useful to help you build resilience, because
even though you can justify your thoughts, it doesn't mean it's valuable to focus on them. We need to really show that to our brain to
reduce its resistance to changing its outlook. This may take some
time; it wasn't like I magically changed my perspective on my sister's
death overnight. You might need weeks or months to work through
this reflection stage and really see and understand how unhelpful
your current outlook is. I recommend continuing journaling on
these reflection questions and let yourself explore the ways in which
this outlook is helping or harming you. You don't have to talk yourself out of these thoughts, just like I don't try to convince myself
that my sister shouldn't be alive right now. I don't want to believe
that. I do think she should still be here. But, there's also a million
different other things I can focus on and choose to believe instead
that serve me far better than dwelling on something I can't change.
So yes—life may be continuing to hit you with unfair setback after
unfair setback and you have every justified reason to feel angry at
someone or something right now. But if these negative thoughts
make you feel and act in ways that only make your life harder and
more miserable, they're not the ones you have to stay stuck on.

A lot of things are tough about being human, but one of the
greatest abilities we have is the ability to redirect our mind to look
at the same circumstance in a different way. That's what I'll teach
you how to do in the following chapters with the third and final
"R" to resilience. First, we'll talk to you about what to do when
you're feeling stuck or too overwhelmed to practice any of these
steps—because I've definitely had those days, too.

7

Cultivating Self Compassion

Once you recognize how much your thinking plays into how you feel and handle situations, and you reflect on how unhelpful it is, it can be tempting to jump straight to judging yourself for being so negative or thinking that way in the first place. "I know I shouldn't think that" is a common thought I hear often from my coaching clients, who take the lessons from the previous chapters and then use them against themselves. I've been guilty of doing this, too.

But you cannot judge and berate yourself into being resilient. It has to begin with compassion for yourself. You're not weak-minded for having negative thoughts—you're human. As I've mentioned, you likely have valid reasons for thinking what you're thinking, and that means it can often take some time to move between the different phases of the 3 Rs, especially the reflec-

You cannot judge and berate yourself into being resilient. It has to begin with compassion for yourself.

tion phase. Even though you now have awareness of what your thoughts are and how they're impacting you, you may still need time to process the whole experience.

In 2020, when I was still living in Australia, I had an appointment scheduled with the US Consulate. My now-husband Nate and

I had spent nine months out of the previous year apart, and I was anxious to get my visa approved so I could move to the United States to be with him. When my consulate appointment in Australia was canceled due to the pandemic setting in, I didn't instantly feel resilient and ready to be proactive. In fact, I took long walks by the bay with my childhood dog, Cooper, while tears streamed from beneath my sunglasses as I listened to Nate's and my shared playlist. I cried a lot. I vented to my parents. I cried some more.

Just like physical wounds, emotional wounds take time to heal. So we need to be compassionate to ourselves through this process. This means giving yourself permission to feel whatever you need to feel, but also being mindful to not start drowning in the difficult feelings. That starts to become self-pity, which has nothing to do with self-compassion. On the other extreme, if we try to push away and prevent ourselves from feeling emotion at all, that turns into self-denial. In this chapter, we'll explore how to embrace the power of self-compassion while avoiding the two extreme ends of the feeling spectrum: self-pity and self-denial. There's a healthy balance in between where resilience can be found.

Studies show that expressing our emotions to others can increase our sense of belonging and help reduce our stress through the empathy and validation other people can provide us. However, if you're in the middle of a major venting session and all your friend is doing is validating how much of a jerk your ex is or how unfair it is that your colleague stole your pitch idea, in the long term, venting to them may actually make you feel worse because they're simply letting you fall further into the beliefs that cause self-pity the most.

The beliefs that cause self-pity the most are what psychologist Martin Seligman calls the "3 Ps": permanence, personal, and pervasiveness. "Permanence" is the idea that you're always going to feel terrible and the difficult situation you're in is never going to improve. This is a common belief to have when you've been hit with a setback that technically is permanent, like the death of a loved one or a diagnosis for a disease that has no cure. The permanence of the circumstance makes it easy to feel like your feelings about it all will be permanently awful, too.

A "personal" belief relates to the idea that the world is personally out to get *you* and you're the only one who has a life this difficult. If you've ever heard a friend say "You just don't understand what I'm going through," they are holding on to a "personal" belief that they are the only person who is experiencing painful emotions that intensely.

"Pervasiveness" is the sneaky belief that one particular loss or setback means everything in your life is now terrible or ruined. Someone with this perspective believes that there's nothing good or worthwhile about life anymore. This thought typically emerges after a terrible or tragic life event.

While the thoughts that cause permanent, personal, or pervasive beliefs may feel true, we now know that our brain finds evidence for what it already believes. So dwelling on them only makes them feel truer, because your brain is constantly scanning to prove why all of these Ps are true. This causes a mountain of self-pity.

While we all feel bad for ourselves sometimes, we don't want it to become the place we live life from. This is because self-pity leads to self-defeating behavior. *"What's the point? I've had a such a crappy week, I might as well skip my gym workout and not bother going to my friend's birthday dinner because my life sucks, and I don't need to hear how great other people's lives are going, and I certainly do not feel like being told to do 10 burpees by my trainer tonight."*

You temporarily get the comfort of lounging on your couch and not having to put any effort into socializing or exercising. Perhaps that night, that's exactly what you needed. However, if you let those choices become a habit, you're missing out on some of the things that are crucial to your long-term mental health and resilience (more on that to come in Chapter 13!) and giving yourself more opportunity to ruminate and dwell on all the things that are "wrong" with your life, which keeps the self-pity cycle going.

Now, I am not trying to tell you to be a stone cold stoic and push away your feelings with fake smiles and pretend "everything is totally fine!" Denying your feelings is just as unhelpful as wallowing in them. When we try to stuff away our feelings and not open up about them at all, we actually intensify the emotion because pushing against it creates more energy. Feelings are meant to be felt, not pushed into a cupboard or covered up with a pretty bow. Also, we can't self-select which emotions we want to feel and which ones we don't. So if denying your emotions is your default way of dealing with them, while you may not feel the depths of grief or pain, you may also notice that you don't feel the heights of joy or happiness. This often leads to feeling apathetic about life and disconnected from yourself and your purpose.

Both self-pity and self-denial sucks away your energy to be resilient. Self-compassion, on the other hand, helps you hold on to your power and ability to be resilient.

The difference is this:

SELF-DENIAL SAYS: "Oh, I'm fine; everything is totally fine."

SELF-PITY SAYS: "This sucks; I can't handle it."

SELF-COMPASSION SAYS: "This is really hard, and I *can* handle it."

Self-compassion acknowledges and allows space for all of your feelings and struggles, but it also believes in your ability to handle it: to grow through it and to figure it out. This subtle difference changes everything. In fact, as a human you are designed to evolve under pressure. There needs to be some sort of tension or

As a human you are designed to evolve under pressure.

struggle in order for your growth to occur. So we don't have to *like* our hard times, but we do have to accept that they are a part of life.

I remember once telling my neighbor the old saying, "I've never met a strong person with an easy past," and he replied, "I've never met someone with an easy past." For years, his comment has stuck with me because of just how true it is. It's easy in a busy world of surface level interactions and highlight reels where people are only showing us what they want us to see online to assume most people have an easy life. But your boss who seems so uptight may also have a niece with cancer or that fitspo influencer who seems to "have it all" may struggle with mental health. No human gets through life scot-free from struggle. Just because we might not see it or know about it, doesn't mean it's not happening.

We are fragile beings living in an unpredictable world where loss, adversity, and setbacks are built into the fabric of our experience. That's what makes self-compassion different from self-pity— self-pity takes hardships and setbacks personally, like we're being targeted by the world or are the "unlucky one." When truthfully, the only unlucky one is the one who's not here to complain how unlucky they are. Self-compassion embraces this. It acknowledges that in one way or another, life is hard for everyone. Period. Accepting this helps us drop our ego that thinks we're entitled to an easy life and connect more with our own humility—that struggle is a part of being human. We'll never be above feeling negative emotion and loss sometimes, no matter how rich, beautiful, or successful we are.

In fact, if you dig beneath it all, you actually don't want to be someone who has never experienced pain or grief. Because we don't grieve because we lost someone, we grieve because we loved someone. People die around us all day, every day, yet we don't grieve them all. We only grieve the people we love. Love is the birthplace of grief. Similarly, we aren't disappointed because we missed out on an opportunity, but because we *cared* about that opportunity.

So if we were to try to strip all uncomfortable emotion out of our lives, we'd also have to strip it of all meaning. To live a life without uncomfortable emotion is to live without caring and connection—which is not really a life at all. Knowing that although it's hard—although your eyes are red and puffy, your tummy is in knots or your heart feels like it's being twisted by a knife—these are uncomfortable emotions you actually want to feel. You naturally don't want to feel happy that your mother has cancer; that your dog is dying; that your boyfriend is being deployed overseas for six months. These are situations we want to think thoughts that make us feel sadness or disappointment about. *"I really hurt seeing my mom so unwell." "I feel so sad I can't snuggle up with my boyfriend right now." "I really wish dogs' lives weren't so short."* All of those are healthy natural human thoughts to have, which cause you to feel these heavy emotions.

Let them. Let yourself feel them, because without these experiences your life will feel hollow, half-lived and half-loved. Compassion makes space for this and helps to balance out the negativity of these experiences by accepting this is the way life goes. There's no life where you still wouldn't have any problems, struggles, or challenges. There's no life where everything always goes your way.

Although emotions like pain, disappointment, stress, or grief are typically called "negative emotions," it's helpful to realize they actually come from the best parts of life, like experiencing love or finding what you're passionate about. There's nothing negative about that. They are simply the price we pay to experience the parts of life that make being a human meaningful.

This reframing is what can prevent us from layering these difficult emotions with the "poor me" story or the idea that we "shouldn't" be feeling disappointed or stressed. Instead, self-compassion gives all of your emotions a landing place to "just be."

Self-compassion gives all of your emotions a landing place to "just be."

I think we are sometimes deluded into believing that had we taken a different path in life or made a different decision, then we'd be happier or not have to struggle at all, but it's simply not true. It'll never be that way because we have a brain that is wired to seek problems and fear threats. Your brain could be in your dream scenario, and it will still be tempted to find the imperfections and problems. I know this because once I finally got the chance to move to the United States with Nate after nearly two long years of back-and-forth long distance, I began to feel sadness over missing my family and stressed about having to start all over again, making new friendships, and familiarizing myself with a new town. In fact, I still feel incredibly sad living so far away from my Mum and Dad, and my fur brother, Charlie. It is my dream to be living with Nate, but I still have thoughts that create difficult emotions because people I care about are far away from me. I could've stayed in Australia at a job and relationship I didn't want to be in, and then I would've had uncomfortable emotions like restlessness and discontent. Both circumstances are hard in their own ways, but this life I've chosen is hard in a way that makes life worth it—the other would've been hard in a way that makes life feel empty.

So rather than wishing away your stress or pain, make space for it. Accept that perhaps if you'd chosen differently, the details of your life may be different, but you'd still have setbacks, struggles and problems to deal with. Reminding yourself of this helps your resilience because you'll stop compounding your struggle with resentment and frustration that life has let you down and is out to get you. Instead, you can step into the acceptance that you live in a world of adversity with a human brain that will naturally create thoughts of struggle and pain. That is the heartbreakingly beautiful experience of being human.

So now that we know why compassion is so powerful during this Reflect stage of resilience, I want to share with you what I call The 3 As to Self-Compassion. I created them as I was reflecting on self-compassion and how easy it is to fall to either side of the self-denial or self-pity spectrum. But these 3 As are simple to remember and hold on to when you're having a tough time. Before we go into proactive mode, it's important we let ourselves be human.

The first "A" is to **acknowledge.** To acknowledge is to let yourself know that you see and recognize your feelings. It sounds like a very simple step, but too many times we want to dismiss our feelings or judge them. Yet various research studies, including one by Dr. Michelle Craske at University of California, show that being able to identify and label what it is you're really feeling is an important first step toward regulating your emotions. So, let go of what you think *should* be feeling and make space for whatever thoughts you recognize are coming to the surface for now (see Miller, 2021, in the Bibliography).

For some of us, our emotional vocabulary can be limited to basic feelings like happy, sad, anxious, and mad, which limits our understanding of what's really going on for us. So with your difficult situation in mind, I want you to quickly Google "feelings list" and read through all the different feelings one can feel, and identify to yourself what it is you're specifically feeling about that situation. You can find the link to my favorite feelings list in the Resources section at the end of the book.

The next step is to open up the Notes section in your phone and start a note with the title "The 3 As to Self-Compassion." Under that title, write "Acknowledge" and copy and paste the link where you found the feelings list—or write down some feelings you notice you often feel from the list I provide in the Resource section of the book. This is to help you remember to practice this step of acknowledging your feelings next time you're struggling. Beneath the link, I want you to write:

"I know you're feeling _____ (insert feeling) right now. I see you. I feel you."

Close your eyes and repeat this mantra to yourself three times as you would to a loved one who's feeling emotional. It sounds like a subtle step, but it's one that helps us stay connected to our human experience rather than trying to escape it.

The second "A" is **accept.** This step is about accepting that there's no way that you get through life without hard moments. It's an important part of keeping us out of Martin Seligman's 3 P beliefs: permanence, personal, and pervasive, so we don't stay feeling like the world is out to get us or our lives will permanently be this bad. Without accepting that life is going to be unfair sometimes, it's difficult to find the resilience to deal with it, as we're too busy arguing against it. Of all of the 3 As, this is the one I personally struggle to keep in mind sometimes—especially as it's so easy these days to compare our worst moments with someone else's highlight reel. But if we can sink back into the more accurate truth that, in one way or another, everyone faces difficulties in life, and that's the way this world is, we stop wasting energy comparing and despairing, and connect with our humility and strength to cope with that reality. I personally like to remind myself that struggle and adversity is a small price to pay for the opportunity to live in this world and experience what it feels like to love and be loved.

So in the Notes app on your phone, beneath your section on "Acknowledge", I want you to write "Accept" and next to it this calming mantra that grounds you back to the truth of this world and helps keep things in perspective during difficult times:

"This human thing is hard for everyone, and that's OK. Dark days like these are the price we pay for the gift of experiencing being alive in this world."

The final "A" is **appreciation.** Appreciate yourself like you would a friend. Appreciation counteracts the tendency to want to judge or resist our feelings in ways that spiral us into self-denial. To find that balance of compassion, we need to practice speaking to ourselves as if we are speaking to someone we care about, because truthfully, you do need to love and care about *you* in order to support yourself through challenges and heartbreaks.

I know it's easy to hold yourself to a higher, and often unrealistic, expectation than you do your loved ones. Maybe you think you should already be over this thing or shouldn't be so torn up about what happened. But as Canadian politician Norm Kelly said, "You can't pour from an empty cup." This kind of judgment puts a perpetual hole in that cup and will never give you anything with which you can care for others, let alone yourself. So appreciating yourself for how well you're doing with your struggle, even if you're struggling way more than you think you should be, is another important step to compassion. Stay present with your struggle as if you were holding its hand and talking to your best friend. That's how we find the courage to keep taking baby steps forward.

It's what I did when I was so hurt and scared about not getting to see Nate again during the pandemic due to so many circumstances beyond my control. I was tempted to judge myself for being so emotional about it. I knew other people were dealing with far worse circumstances at the time. But that judgment made me feel even worse, which made me even moodier and caused more tension between Nate and me. So instead, I remembered that it was okay that I was really struggling with this. It was okay that I was crying so much. In fact, my little mantra was "I can do things crying"! When I got out for a walk with my dog every day, I gave myself permission to feel what I needed to while still doing what I could. I know that was so beneficial to my mental health, which put me on a faster track to accepting our current reality and finding ways to make the most of it. Nate and I had FaceTime date nights, and I even wrote a love song that I found a freelance singer to record for me, and I surprised Nate with it over Zoom. His reaction was priceless, and we ended up playing it as part of our wedding ceremony a few years later. That's what this step of self-compassion helped me create.

So when you notice you're tempted to judge your feelings or lose belief in your capacity to get through whatever hard thing you're dealing with, here is what you need to remember—and what I want you to write in the 3 As note section on your phone:

"Appreciate—No matter how many tears or counseling sessions you need to go to, I am going to love you the whole way through it. You can get through this."

Keep this note on your phone and open it up whenever you feel yourself beginning to spiral into self-pity or denial, and you need a shoulder to lean on. I've also created a free printout of the 3 As in my downloadable resources. I suggest putting it up on

your bedroom mirror or wall to remind yourself daily of these three steps when you're going through a rough patch. Just scan this QR code to instantly access it.

While I do want you to reach out to family, friends, and professional support as much as you need, never forget to be your own shoulder to lean on, too. Give your emotions a soft place to land and be healthily processed by using these 3 As: acknowledge, accept, and appreciate. Hold the space for your life experience and whatever emotions come with it. As hard as it is sometimes, never lose sight of the fact that pain and loss come from the parts of life that make all this struggle worth it.

8

Learning How to Forgive

In Chapter 6, we reflected on how blame and bitterness only punishes you. It makes you feel and act in ways that perpetuates your own suffering. After my sister died, I could have argued all day long about how the police "should" have done a better job being honest and seeking justice and how the driver who killed my sister "should" be in jail. My family fought hard for justice but the Thai legal system had made up its mind—no charges would be laid initially, case closed. I could stay mad at that man forever, but for what? It wouldn't change a thing. If I stayed mad, my sister wouldn't suddenly be alive again. The man who crashed into her wouldn't be in prison. And I'd just trap myself in my own prison of anger and misery.

Who wants to live like that? I deserve more than a life of misery and so do you. No matter how unfair the cards are that life has dealt you—whether it be through the actions of someone else or pure bad luck—you'll never grow through what you go through until you let go of blame and choose forgiveness.

You'll never grow through what you go through until you let go of blame and choose forgiveness.

Choosing forgiveness—to let go of any anger or resentment from a past wrongdoing—can be incredibly hard, especially if you haven't received closure, like me, or if the person you're wanting to forgive hasn't apologized. When we've been impacted by someone's unjust or spiteful behavior, we can feel shocked that they're able to get away with their actions. It's easy to want to hold on to the blame until you receive an apology from them or see karma come along and bite them on the butt. We think that will bring some sort of satisfaction that'll make it easier to let go or move past what they did. And the truth is, it can. Seeking justice can bring more closure to your pain to help release the blame and anger a little.

However, the problem with waiting for closure before you're willing to forgive is that you're putting your power back into the hands of something you cannot control. You're now dependent on that person being willing to own their mistakes and apologize or for the police to properly do their investigation and charge someone accordingly. If you're waiting for something external to happen in order to forgive, you're surrendering your own power to be resilient.

So while choosing to forgive is something that is a personal choice that is entirely up to you, in this chapter, I will walk you through four key truths about why forgiveness is important. There are some misconceptions about why we shouldn't forgive others that keeps us holding onto our anger as if it's serving us in some way, but these four truths will reveal why choosing to hold a grudge only punishes you and how much more power you gain back over your life, once you do choose to forgive.

Truth #1: Holding a grudge only makes your life harder

Holding a grudge can sometimes feel like a useful way to get revenge. Perhaps your colleague took credit for one of your ideas at work, so you stop inviting them to team lunch. Or maybe your doctor misdiagnosed you, so you start being short-tempered with them. It can feel tempting to stay angry at someone as a way to get back at them.

However, seeking revenge is about as useful as the "k" in the word knife. Because other people don't feel *our* feelings. That person you're holding a grudge against does not feel your anger; they only experience their interpretation of your behavior. You can't control how they choose to interpret how you act. So you might be putting a ton of energy into trying to make their life more miserable, but they could still choose to think, "I feel sorry for Sarah, she clearly hasn't moved on," or "I'm bigger than letting Zane's actions get the better of me," and so they don't feel any of your anger or negativity.

The only person who truly suffers when you hold a grudge is you. When we let our pain harden into bitterness and hold a grudge against the world for it, we also start adding to the suffering in our lives and those around us. We start to act similarly to the person who hurt us to get back at them—but those actions often affect others in our life, too. We complain more. Become more pessimistic. More judgmental. Quicker to blame and shame. We dismiss the good and dwell on the bad.

For example, I was working with Bianca, whose best friend, Eva, lost her job one year before. Eva was told it was because the company missed out on a big deal that she was responsible for closing. Eva is deeply resentful toward her boss because she felt it was a lack of communication between company departments that let them down and that she was just being used as the scapegoat. She was consumed by her anger, and she couldn't talk about anything else. Bianca missed the old Eva; since being fired, Eva constantly complained about her boss and brainstormed about how she'll get back at him through litigation. Bianca worked hard to keep her brain in a strong and positive place, so she worked with me as her life coach on the best way to talk with Eva about this. Bianca decided to

gently tell Eva that while she loved her and understood how difficult losing her job was for her, she was feeling overwhelmed by the
negativity and needed to take a step back.

Perhaps you can relate to a situation just like this with a friend
or family member of your own: you try to have a catch up chat on
the phone but all they want to do is rant about how terrible their
ex-husband is for leaving, telling you all the same negative things
about him that they told you last week. You feel for them, but given
you're trying to stay in a good head space, before long, it's tempting
to stop taking their calls in order to protect your own mental health.
That's what holding grudges costs you, not only your own relationship with yourself but your relationships with other people you love.

So whether you want to forgive someone in your life is up to
you. But please don't make that choice from believing that being
bitter at them is useful. It's not. Being vengeful makes you lose power
over what true revenge is: moving onwards and upwards from whatever pain or struggle that person has caused you.

Truth #2: We were never promised a fair life

Something unfair will happen to every single person in their lifetime. Some people more than others. And I do want to acknowledge that first and foremost. You may have been born into
circumstances that have been stacked against you since you were
young. Whether it's a broken home, loss of caretakers in early
childhood, war and violence, abuse, poverty—it's heartbreaking
to conceive of the adversity you and our fellow humans may have
to go through in life. This world can be so unfair. And it's okay
to want to stick your middle finger up at the world and be so mad
at how cruel it can be. Those moments are natural and understandable, and you can have as many of those moments as
you need throughout your life journey. That's when the tools of

self-compassion that we explored in the last chapter are most help-ful. However, we've also seen how living in that bitter place of stay-ing angry at the world for an unfair reality you cannot change only creates more suffering for yourself in the long term. So while I still have moments of anger for my sister being taken so young—or sometimes simply at minor annoyances like the weather delay-ing my plane or spilling coffee down my shirt before a keynote presentation—I know that spiraling into how much I hate how unfair life can be only makes things worse.

So what I want to share with you is the mini-pep talk that I give myself (and my coaching clients) when I notice that rather than just having temporary feelings of intense anger and frustra-tion about an unfair situation, it's becoming an entire mindset from which we're living life. Here's a powerful question to ask: Do you remember how before we came to Earth, we signed the document that said "Your life will be fair and easy, and everything will go your way!" Yeah, me neither. Because it didn't happen. Unfortunately, we are not guaranteed fairness in this life. We've hit the jackpot of a lifetime getting to experience this world for such a fleeting time, and although not all of it is wonderful, not all of it is terrible, either. Yes, we live in a world where there are people who lie, cheat, steal, and kill. But we also live in a world where we can see the sunrise, video chat to a loved one on the other side of the world, where flow-ers grow through dirt, where the waves wash against the shore, where we can turn on taps and get fresh water, and where there are thousands of people dedicating their lives to finding ways to help those who can't. There's ice cream and hot coffee, and puppies and airplanes that let us explore mountain tops and snowy valleys. There's teachers, doctors, soldiers, nurses, firefighters, and people who dedicate their lives to serving others and their country. There are selfish people and selfless people. There's winter and there's sum-mer. There's night and there's day. Everything about this world is contrast; for every circumstance we want to interpret as awful and unfair, there's a circumstance or experience out there that we have every reason to be celebrating, appreciating, and living in awe of. We do not want to miss that beauty because we're too busy resisting the ugly parts of the world.

Being part of the world's healing and resilience begins with letting go of all expectations for life to be easier and accepting the fact that it isn't. *"The world isn't fair, and that's okay."* It's okay, because the alternative of resisting it only makes you suffer more. It's also okay, because it's not what happens to us but how we choose to respond that dictates our experience in this world.

I've found I'm stronger when I accept that there are things in the world that I *want* to interpret as negative; but I don't make that mean something is wrong with the world. Because that only makes me suffer; instead I choose to bring my own meaning that perhaps this *is* the purpose of life. That the hard things, the unwanted things, the outright awful painful heart wrenching things aren't here to take away from our human experience, but are a way to add to it if we choose to step up and take responsibility for what we can change and learn from for the better. That's a choice we each get to make: to turn our struggles into opportunities for contribution and growth.

I realized that is a defining factor in whether adversity makes us bitter or better. Holocaust survivor Eddie Jaku spoke of how he spent his life carrying so much pain from the trauma he endured, but he realized that if he leaned into what his loss and pain could teach him, he could use that to help others process their own trauma. He stopped arguing against the unfair horrors of his past, and looked toward using those lessons to create a better future for himself, his family, and now through his own book, *The Happiest Man on Earth*, for generations to come.

So if we can each channel our inner Eddie and accept that life is going to be unfair for all of us in different ways, we get so much more capacity to contribute to the good contrast of this world rather than the darkness. We do not have to like the circumstances we are given, but what matters is who you choose to be in response to those circumstances. I say this with all of the love of my heart. I refuse to let you give away your power by resisting against the hard parts of your life. You cannot move past what's happened to you until you make peace with the fact it did happen. Let go of resistance. Let go of the judgment against the world for being unfair. Let go of the blame. Accepting that life was never meant to be easy actually makes it a little easier to handle.

> *We do not have to like the circumstances we are given, but what matters is who you choose to be in response to those circumstances.*

Truth #3: Forgiveness isn't condoning what happened, it's setting yourself free

Sometimes forgiveness can be difficult because it feels like doing it would communicate that you condone the behavior of the person who hurt you. For example, if you grew up with a father who verbally abused you and your mother, it could feel impossible to say, "Dad, it's okay for the way you used to yell at Mom and me, it's all good." And that is something I totally understand. However, forgiveness isn't about letting someone else off the hook. It's letting *you* off the hook. When you forgive someone, you are not saying that you are okay with inappropriate or unjust behavior. You are not being weak or letting the other person "win." When you choose to forgive, you are simply releasing the resentment and anger that is causing you so much suffering. It is setting yourself free by accepting the reality that we are all human with flaws and pain that can make us act in ways that cause more pain. As Rabbi Yehuda Berg once said, "hurt people hurt people." Some people never learn how to handle their own pain or wounds, so they unfortunately act in ways that perpetuate the destructive cycle. You cannot change that reality for them, but you can set yourself free from that cycle by choosing to forgive them. And the beautiful thing is, it's a gift you can give to yourself at any moment. Even if the person never apologizes or you never see them again.

I know this because I am not living with anger at the guy who killed my sister, and I've never spoken a word to him. I do not condone his actions of reckless driving. But I will not let his actions determine the kind of person I am in the world. That is my choice. That is why I choose acceptance. I choose forgiveness. I choose to end the fight against what *should* be and learn to embrace what is, so I can move forward in a way that I am proud of and experience more joy in my life.

In fact, here's a letter I wrote a few years after I lost my sister. I never actually sent it to him; I wouldn't have a clue where to find him. Nor do I have any desire to. But it was therapeutic to write, and I am including it in this chapter for anyone who's in so much pain and resentment at the world for what they've been through that forgiveness feels beyond reach. I hope this letter helps you inch your way closer to forgiveness and the freedom that comes with it.

To the guy who caused my sister's accident,

I am writing this to you. You were never sorry. You never admitted fault. You never reached out or gave compassion to my family. You are everything I don't want to be. But I choose to forgive, not to relieve you but to set me free. For I have a whole life ahead of me, and I will not spend a second of it on hating what you took away from me, but instead loving what you never can: the essence of my sister. Her legacy. Her spirit. Her passion for life. These live on in all the hearts she touched. Most especially mine. You broke it in a way I never imagined, but you also taught me the true strength of who I can be.

I do not wish this pain upon you, because I do not wish more suffering in the world. I do wish however, if you ever cause someone such sorrow again, you give what any decent human being would: love. A hug. An apology. It does not take back what happened. But it does keep someone believing in humanity when they have every reason not to. Thankfully I still had the greatest reason to: my love for my sister. That will always outshine anything you could ever do in this world. A million times over. So forgiveness I choose—not because you deserve it, but because Nicole does. She deserves a little sister empowered to live life large enough for the two of us—and not a single part of that involves you.

Now it's time for you to write about what forgiveness might look like for you. Take out a notebook or the Notes app on your phone, and write down your answers to each of the following questions. If any resistance comes up as you start to write your answers, that's okay. Don't judge yourself or push it away, just try out opening your mind up to the possibility of forgiving this person—even if you're not quite there yet, these questions may help you inch your way closer to finding that sense of peace you're looking for.

1. Where in your life do you notice you're holding a grudge? Where do you feel resentful or vengeful?

2. Think of something that happened that you still feel angry or bitter about. What part of you resists forgiving the person or people who hurt you? What fears or worries do you have if you chose to forgive them?

3. In what way is holding on to this grudge making your life harder? What important things does it distract you from or make you miss out on (e.g. *I miss out on going to social gatherings that this person goes to, I spend a lot of time thinking about getting back at them,* etc.)?

4. How could your life feel freer if you chose to forgive this person?

5. Are you open to the idea of one day forgiving this person? Let's practice it below. Fill in the blank in the sentence below with someone you want to forgive. See how it feels when you write out this sentence.

   I choose to forgive ____ (insert person's name), not because they are free from fault, but because I want to be free from the anger that I carry so I can find more peace and power over my life. I am worthy of that freedom and love.

6. If you want to dive deeper into forgiving someone and feel you have more you want to express to them, practice writing a letter to this person, using the one I shared above as an example. The purpose of this letter is to help you let your anger out one last time and release the burden that it weighs on you. Aim to write at least seven to ten sentences about how you're feeling toward this person, what you wish was different about what happened, and why you're choosing to move forward for your own sake of peace and freedom. Once you finish writing this letter, close your eyes and take three deep breaths, and with each breath out, feel the heaviness of the grudge flow out of your body. Whether you give this

letter to the person or not, there is power in writing it and
opening your mind up to what you can gain through choosing
to forgive.

Beyond these writing exercises, continue to have simple conversations in your mind, where every time you notice your thoughts
wanting to blame or dwell on what happened, you simply remind
yourself, "I am bigger than this experience. I will not let this
define me. I choose forgiveness and to let go." Your ego may want
to resist doing so. But I hope your heart finds the courage to
extend forgiveness to those who deserve it least. Because remember, only *you* feel your feelings. And there's no better feeling than
peace.

Truth #4: You can't self-improve from self-loathing

There's one last type of forgiveness that needs to be mentioned,
and sometimes it's the hardest one to do: self-forgiveness. Initially, guilt can be helpful in indicating where you acted out of
alignment with your values and who you want to be. It's your
internal moral compass saying, "Hey, you did something wrong
here," and can lead to productive action like apologizing or seeking professional help. However, when you begin to believe that
because of your mistakes there's something wrong *with* you, you've
let guilt turn into shame, and shame is never a helpful emotion.
It causes us to hide, turn away, and spiral further into rumination. *"You idiot, you messed up the whole presentation for your boss
by dropping that glass of water all over the laptop!"* or *"Why did you
have that extra drink and then text your ex? You look so desperate
and pathetic now!"*

Shaming ourselves leads to self-loathing, as if making mistakes is inexcusable. Yet humans by design are flawed and bound to make mistakes. Including you. Allow space for your humanness. It doesn't mean you abdicate responsibility for something wrong that you did. But when you continue to beat yourself up for it as if there's something wrong with you, you spiral further into self-defeating behavior. You cannot learn and grow from a mistake while you're still busy berating yourself for it.

Instead, resilience means replacing self-criticism with self-compassion and curiosity. For example, rather than judging yourself as weak for texting your ex, who you know is no good for you, lean in with curiosity about the thoughts and feelings that lead you to making that choice. Be curious about what you were thinking right before you texted him. What need were you trying to fulfill? What feeling were you trying to escape? Open up and explore these questions to gain insight into what you need to heal and how you can choose differently next time those thoughts and feelings come up.

Instead, resilience means replacing self-criticism with self-compassion and curiosity.

One of my clients felt a lot of shame after being caught shoplifting. In our session, she said, "I knew better than to do that!!" And the truth is, she did know better. But when she sits there berating herself for that, she's missing out on doing the powerful work of exploring what was beneath her urge to shoplift. Because despite being brought up to know that stealing is wrong, she still did it. I worked with her to lean in and figure out why: What need was she trying to fill by taking those clothes? Was she trying to seek more thrill in her life? Rebel against her upbringing? Feel more in control? We had a deep discussion around all of this, which helped her reveal to herself that she's not crazy or damaged, she had just been feeling bored and unfulfilled in her life recently and wanted to push the boundaries to feel more thrill and novelty. She wanted to stop being a "good girl" and take more risks. This realization was so impactful for her because with this discovery, we could help her find healthier ways to bring novelty into her life that didn't cause consequences or go against her character. With new insights and understanding, she can choose differently next time. That's the power of curiosity over criticism: curiosity teaches while criticism cripples.

Sometimes, we can feel also shame and give into self-loathing if something terrible happened to someone we love that we thought we could control. For example, maybe your nephew had to go to the hospital after getting in a car accident on his way to soccer practice, and you are feeling guilty for not getting home earlier and driving him yourself. If this is you, surrender to the fact that this world is far bigger than we are. We couldn't have possibly known that things would unfolded like they did. It's not fair to judge yourself for past choices like this from where you are now. You didn't have the same insight and perspective at that moment. And even if you had made a different choice—like arriving home earlier or not making a commitment that afternoon to prevent you from driving your nephew—you still don't know if that would've changed the overall outcome. We'll never know, which is why it's simply not helpful to keep spinning over it. The world is bigger than us and our actions.

Because I suggested my sister go to Thailand on vacation, I felt so much guilt. What if I hadn't suggested she go there? We could "what if" ourselves all day long and beat ourselves up for doing what we did, but that only leads to more loss and suffering in an already difficult situation. We cannot change the past. But we can change the future by what we can learn from the past. I couldn't save my sister's life, but I chose to share the lessons I learned from her death about travel safety to help save someone else's. I never would have found the

We cannot change the past. But we can change the future by what we can learn from the past.

strength to do that if I hadn't forgiven myself and surrendered to the reality that I can't control every outcome.

All each of us can do is make the best choice we can with the information we have available at that moment. Grant yourself the space to make mistakes and detours in this life, knowing that they can still be a valuable experience when viewed through the lens of curiosity and compassion. Forgive yourself; it's the only way forward from here.

I've written this chapter not to pretend that forgiveness is easy, but that it is always possible—so long as we hold on to these four truths:

1. Holding a grudge only makes your life harder.
2. We were never promised a fair life.
3. Forgiveness isn't condoning what happened, it's setting yourself free.
4. You can't self improve from self loathing.

Or if you're a fan of a powerful metaphor like myself, there is a famous saying by Buddha that I think sums up the biggest reason to let go and forgive: "Holding on to anger is like grasping a hot coal with the intent of throwing it at someone else; you are the one who gets burned."

While these can take time to work through and accept, I hope by guiding you through each of these four truths, you are more open minded to the power of forgiveness and why it's worth the effort it can take to get there. Whether it's keeping in mind that holding a grudge only weighs you down and can push away those we love most, or that forgiveness isn't making what happened okay, it's simply setting yourself free to move forward with peace in your heart, I hope you've found some helpful perspectives to support you along your own journey of forgiveness, one brave step at a time.

In the fourth part of this book, you'll learn the final step in the 3 R strategy that I used to be resilient enough to help me transform my heartbreaks and struggles into something purposeful—so you can do the same in your life, too.

PART 4

Redirect Your Mind

9

Empower Yourself Through Deliberate Questions

Now that you know how to recognize your own thoughts rather than believe that they're facts, understand which biases of your brain to look out for, and also when to reflect upon the impact of your thoughts, I can now introduce you to the third and final R in the three steps to resilience: **Redirect.** This is the step where you learn how to redirect your mind to perspectives that will help you turn life's sucker punches into growth-worthy experiences that you gain something from. I know this is always possible, even in the worst of circumstances, because it's exactly what I managed to do with the tragedy of losing my sister. I love teaching the third R the most because it's where most of the growth and transformation can happen.

So far, we've learned that changing our lives begins by changing our minds. We can't create purposeful outcomes from our hardships if we're not focusing on the things that give us the peace, strength, and determination to do so. On autopilot, our brain tends to dwell on the opposite: the losses, the pain, the negatives, and the things you can't change. But the good news is, you are not at the mercy of your automatic brain, thanks to your prefrontal cortex. Remember that's the part of the brain that we can take conscious control of and tell it what to focus on, on purpose! It's where we have the freedom of choice. The prefrontal cortex is involved in every stage of the 3 Rs—it helps us recognize our thoughts and reflect upon their impact—but the prefrontal cortex is really about to show off its amazing powers in this final step. This is where you're going to dive deeper into your own creativity, resourcefulness, curiosity, and wisdom to help you find more empowering thoughts so you can create better outcomes from any situation life throws at you.

So, *how* do we stop ourselves from spiraling further into negativity? When your brain is in a negative place, positive thoughts tend to rebound right off. Kara came to our session devastated that she didn't make it through the final audition for a Broadway show. She'd been hustling hard for the last ten years to make her Broadway dream come true while working as physician's assistant at a dental office. The producers had seemed positive about her chances at landing a leading role, and she'd spent the last three weeks getting herself pumped up to finally making it happen! Yet, the day before her final audition, she woke up with a sore throat and stuffy nose. She couldn't believe her bad luck at the timing of it. She still went to the audition, but by that point her voice wasn't much more than a croak. She got a disappointing call a day later, with the producers saying, "We're sorry, but we've chosen to go in another direction."

I could feel the heaviness of her heart through my computer screen as she sat in front of me on our Zoom session. "I'm just not cut out for this. I swear it's all rigged against me—how can I be *so* unlucky to get sick the day before the biggest break of my career?!" she said to me. From my bird's-eye view of what was happening, I could see that she still had a lot going for her with more auditions lined up, and this was just an inevitable part of the journey that every performer faced at some time. I saw it time and time again with my sister and her dancing auditions. No one's trajectory to success is straightforward, and I could see that Kara could gain self-belief from recognizing that being a finalist for a lead role in a Broadway show is a major feat. Yet, as a coach I've learned if you start sharing your own perspective too soon, that person is typically quick to get dismissive or defensive. Even if your intentions are well intended and there is merit in the advice or thoughts you're sharing. I mean no one likes being told what to do, let alone what to think! Instead, I've found the magic lies in helping people find those thoughts for themselves—which is a skill I'll teach you in this chapter. You'll learn how to stop the spiraling and start inspiring your mind with thoughts that ignite the strength you need to take resilient action toward healing and growing, using a proven strategy that works every time: asking yourself empowering questions.

This strategy is a great way to get your brain to start practicing thinking positively. Empowering questions are questions that are purposely worded to prompt your mind to instantly be more positive, more future focused, and curious about what you're learning from a circumstance rather than dwelling on what you've lost. You can practice this anytime to instantly cut through any negative thinking and open your mind back up to fresh perspectives that you can't see when you're in the fog of doom and gloom.

This strategy is a simple yet powerful way to gain control back over your mind, because your brain is a question-answering machine. Finding answers to questions and solving problems is what your brain is designed to do. It hates having an open loop in its circuitry; it always wants to find an answer to a question so it can close the loop and feel more certainty. Also, asking your brain a deliberate question immediately switches your brain off autopilot and engages your prefrontal cortex, where you have the ability to think on purpose and step back and see the bigger picture of what's going on.

The key word here is to ask a *deliberate* question, because if you pay attention, you'll actually notice we tend to ask ourselves questions all day long, especially when something bad happens. They often sound like, "Why does my life suck so much?" or "Why am I so unlucky?" or "What's wrong with me?" I call these dead end questions because they come unconsciously from your automatic brain and only prompt your brain to spiral further into unhelpful thoughts and feelings.

Try practicing it now. Close your eyes and quietly ask yourself, "Why am I so unlucky?" What thoughts do you notice automatically appear in your brain? It might sound like, "You're not strong enough!" or "You've never been a winner!" or "You're not destined for much in life!" Our subconscious brain can be a little dramatic, that's for sure! But if we're not paying attention, that's the place we'll respond to setbacks from: our subconscious mind and all its fearful and limited beliefs.

We already ask our brain questions all day long; we've just been asking the wrong ones. Unhelpful questions lead to unhelpful thoughts, feelings and actions. In fact, world famous life coach and motivational speaker Tony Robbins agrees; he wrote in his book, *Awaken the Giant Within*: "The quality of your life is a direct reflection of the quality of the questions you are asking yourself."

Better outcomes from losses and setbacks begin by asking ourselves better questions.

Deliberate questions are what we use to purposely direct our attention and take control over our focus, which in turn determines our feelings and actions. Better outcomes from losses and setbacks begin by asking ourselves better questions.

Here's a list of my top five resilience-building questions to ask your brain on purpose when struggling with a loss or setback. Take out the Notes app on your phone or grab your journal. Write down each of these questions on a new page, titled "Deliberate Questions." Or scan the QR code for access to a 3 Rs worksheet using these deliberate questions. This way, you have them on hand whenever you need to redirect your mind to better handle an unexpected struggle or setback.

1. What can I learn from this to help myself or someone else?
2. How can I turn this setback into a comeback?
3. What would I say to support a friend who was going through this?
4. How does my future self five years from now likely think about this?
5. How could this situation be happening *for* me?

Now, given our brain is naturally quite lazy (remember the good old motivational triad in Chapter 5), its instinct might be to reply "I don't know" or "nothing," but don't let the little toddler fool you. That's your brain just responding on autopilot, so simply ask yourself the question again and be still with yourself for a moment to see what comes up. If you're really struggling to come up with anything, take a guess. So often we're telling ourselves "I don't know" because we fear saying the wrong thing (thanks, school, for only praising us for getting answers right!). But there's no right or wrong in these answers; there's just your truth. So when you tell yourself, "just take a guess," it can help release any self-judgment because a guess by definition is exactly that: it's just a guess. There's no pressure to be right, so you can access more of your creativity and the brainstorming part of your brain, which is really resourceful when you give it a chance to get going!

If there's any resistance to answering these questions because you're thinking something like, "There's *no* way this could be happening for me!" take a breath and go back to the Reflect stage of the 3 Rs. Remember why we're doing this: not to blame you for what's happened, but to give control over how it impacts you now. By searching for more helpful thoughts through these questions, you are not calling your current thoughts invalid, but you can choose to stop focusing on them. Give yourself time to work through these questions—some of them may be more relevant to your situation than others, and that's okay. But there is a reason I've chosen each of these questions. Let's break them down one by one.

Question 1: "What can I learn from this to help myself or someone else?"

The question "What can I learn from this to help myself or someone else?" is most helpful in situations when you don't necessarily want to feel positive about what you've been through, but finding the lessons can help you make it a purposeful experience that you can grow from.

I was coaching Genevieve, a woman in her thirties who had just been diagnosed with multiple sclerosis (MS). She looked back at me with eyes filled with fear and helplessness. She was worried that she was going to become immobile and dependent before she'd found a life partner. "Who could possibly want me if I can barely walk or see properly? I am so scared this disease is going to take over me, and I won't get to travel like I've always wanted to."

As she settled down from her tears at the start of the session, I simply asked, "What are you learning from all of this so far?" She at first joked that she should just give up now and move to a cabin in the middle of nowhere, but she knew that was a little dramatic. So together we began to brainstorm three lessons she'd learned from the diagnosis so far. Here is the list she ended up writing:

1. I'm learning so far to appreciate the health that I do have a whole lot more than I have been. I know there are people who have physical ailments their whole lives; at least I got thirty-five years from this body before having to deal with something like this.

2. I am learning to be more proactive about taking care of my body; I'm always pushing myself at work with late nights, early mornings, skipping workouts, grabbing food at the fast-food store downstairs because I don't have time to cook. This diagnosis is a wake-up call that this all needs to change.

3. I'm learning I need to trust others more. Sometimes I feel like I should just figure out everything on my own and shut people out, but I could really lean on my sister a little more throughout this; she's a nurse, and I know she'll know a lot more about this than I do.

Upon reflection on her list, Genevieve could see that as unwanted as this diagnosis was, it was already beginning to highlight things to her that she'd been pushing aside, including her own health. Being a high achiever at work was always her priority, and now her body was telling her otherwise. She realized her current lifestyle was unsustainable, and in a way she knew that, but she'd been ignoring the warning signs until she was hit with this diagnosis. She told me, "I guess this is teaching me to bring better balance back into my life so I'm not just hustling hard for my career, but also taking care of myself—I won't be able to ignore that anymore now with this diagnosis. I'll need to make room for healthier choices, not just the choices that save me time for work, and I can see how that's a good thing long-term." I could tell she was naturally still feeling some angst about the diagnosis and what it could mean for her long term, but I could also feel she was calmer about the situation overall when she realized the diagnosis was fast tracking her to making better decisions for her well-being that she inevitably was going to need to do. There was less fear and resentment as these lessons helped her gain back a sense of control over her experience of her diagnosis. This is why "What can I learn from this to help myself or someone else?" is such a great question; it opens you up to leaning into the experience and the lessons we can gain from it, rather than shutting them down in worry or shame.

I also purposefully included a second part to the question—"or someone else?"—because sometimes it might be too late to save ourselves from a certain situation, but is there something you can do to help save someone else from it so at least your struggle becomes purposeful.

Katie Shatusky, cofounder of Thumbs Up, a youth mental health and suicide prevention charity, is an amazing example of how you can take the lessons from a painful loss and use it purposefully to save others. Without any warning, she lost her beloved grandfather to suicide. Devastated by his passing and the fact that no one knew that her grandfather was silently living with mental illness due to the taboo about speaking up about it, Katie made the brave decision to do something with her grief. Out for a run one day around her small town, Katie realized how much better going out for a run helped her feel, mentally, physically, and emotionally. Learning how many people feel too afraid to reach out for mental health support and how few support resources there actually were in her local community, she decided to bring together her town for a 5k fun run and start Thumbs Up, named in honor of her Grandpa Bob, who was always giving others a thumbs up. What started as a small community event has now grown into a successful not-for-profit organization that's raised over one million dollars to help fund suicide prevention programs for youth. Katie wants to introduce these mental health resources and support at a young age so no one grows up to become the next Grandpa Bob.

Although Katie's story is very inspiring, please don't think that your way of contributing the lessons from your losses has to be as big as starting up your own charity. It can be as simple as helping out someone who's going through a similar struggle that you've been through and giving them advice on how to better navigate it—like sharing with your niece who is heartbroken after being rejected from her dream college how you went through the same rejection only to end up at a college you love and finding the love of your life there! Or doing a weekly vlog about your IVF journey to help other women also going through it. Or maybe it's organizing a surprise portrait painting of your sister's beloved dog who just passed away as you know how it feels to love a furry member of the family and how much those keepsakes mean once they're gone.

So if you're struggling with a situation where it's too late to use the lessons your adversity has taught you to save yourself or someone else from a painful loss, look forward to the future and out into your community. Whether it's via an in-person event, an online blog, a podcast, an article in your local paper, social media, a charitable organization, or a simple phone call to a friend, there are countless ways these days to raise awareness and make a difference to help others through the lessons we learn from our losses.

Question 2: How can I turn this setback into a comeback?

Anytime you're tempted to keep beating yourself up for messing up, asking "How can I turn this setback into a comeback" is a game changer. As we've learned, there's no upside to focusing on the past once you've learned a lesson from it. So this question is the fastest way to get your mind future-focused and action-oriented about what you can do *now* to move forward.

A great way to answer this question is to write. Open a new page in your notebook or Notes app on your phone and write out everything you can do to help turn this setback into your comeback. Some ideas include:

1. A friend you can call to first of all let out your feelings and frustrations about what happened. Remember, sometimes we need to let it all out before we can begin to sort it out. Once you've done that and you're ready to move forward, then begin to brainstorm:

2. People you can ask for feedback

3. Mentors you can seek advice from

4. Research you can do online to learn more about what to improve upon

5. Courses or classes you can sign up for to build your skills

6. Coaches or professionals you can hire for professional support

7. Weekly habit goals of how often you want to practice getting better at a particular skill set that you need to succeed

Remember, failure isn't fatal, it's how you respond to it that counts. And I mean, who doesn't love a good comeback story?!

Question 3: What would I say to support a friend who was going through this?

We are often our own harshest critic. We berate ourselves for making mistakes or struggling with something that we'd never hold against someone else. Especially not people we care about. Self-judgment and resistance only make things harder. The quickest way to step out of this self-judgment is to ask yourself, "What would I say to a friend in the exact same situation?" We tend to be way more compassionate and understanding of our friends and family than we are ourselves. But guess what? You deserve the same level of compassion and understanding when you're struggling, too.

I was coaching Drew, a law student who studied hard for his midterm exam and got a D. He was telling me how much he felt like giving up, because what was the point? He felt that if he couldn't make it in grad school, he wouldn't make it in the real world as a lawyer. When I asked him this question, his response was entirely different! "Oh, I'd tell him not to stress—it's just one exam and one grade doesn't define your whole future. We've all had exams not go according to plan. Just keep going and ask for more help."

What a far more resilient and empowering perspective to take on board and one that Drew was every bit as worthy of hearing.

So we really need to stop the double standards! We allow other people to make mistakes and struggle, and we need to give ourselves the same permission. You do not need to be unrelentingly flawless at all times. If it's okay for other people to struggle, it's okay for you, too. So the next time you recognize you're judging yourself or expecting yourself to be more than human, ask yourself, "What would I tell my friend?" and then give yourself the same empathy and support. You are worthy of it.

Question 4: How does my future self five years from now likely think about this?

So much of our stress about a situation comes from our brain catastrophizing how detrimental the situation is going to be to our lives long term. We can let stressful situations that are usually minor grow bigger in our minds, so much so that we lose perspective on the big picture of life. Even bigger things like losing your job, getting a serious medical diagnosis, going through a divorce—at first there is a period where our brain is disoriented as it tries to catch up with our new unexpected circumstances. But even through something that involves a huge life change, asking yourself, "How will I think about this in five years' time?" can help settle your brain down and gain perspective you can't see when you're stuck dwelling on the present.

Rebecca had been working hard to become a junior partner at the accounting firm where she'd been working for the last six years. Late nights, early starts, extra training programs and courses—you name, she'd gone the extra mile to be a stand-out option to her bosses. Announcement day came, and Rebecca's name was not called out. It went to her colleague who was also very hard working but did also happen to be the partner's son in-law. She was venting all of her frustration to me during our coaching session. "I worked harder than anyone else and they chose *him*?! I'll now have to wait until another partner position opens up, and who knows when that will be?! My whole career is going down the drain!" I agreed with her that while the choice did seem biased and a big deal at that moment, I asked her how she was going to think about it in five years' time. "Oh, five years from now I know I will have made partner at the firm. Maybe I'll even be a mother and married and not anywhere near as worried about all the politics of this place as there'll be a whole lot more to my life than just work by then."

And that's exactly what I wanted her to remember: while it sucked she wouldn't get junior partner on the timeline she wanted, it didn't mean it was never going to happen, and I didn't want her wasting her energy moping over that so much that she stopped making space for other opportunities and experiences that made her life meaningful, like family and relationships. I just needed her to time travel into the future to be able to gain that insight.

This question "How will my future self think about this in five years?" is the equivalent of what astronauts say about how much perspective they gain looking back down on Earth from space. Seeing how small Earth really is and how vast the universe is, it helps to remember that nothing matters quite as much as it may seem. Everything in life is impermanent, including *life*. Zooming forward to your five-years-from-now self, you can better step into that perspective of seeing the bigger picture and understanding that although things are hard now, you will likely barely remember this setback or be in such a different place with it that you're able to understand why it happened the way it did.

Try this approach with this simple journaling exercise:

1. Take a moment to think about yourself five years ago today. Now spend a few minutes writing about your life back then, in your notebook or your preferred writing app.

For extra prompts to really help you connect with your past self from five years ago, include journaling on details such as:

2. How old were you?
3. What's changed in your life since then, in terms of job, location, and/or relationships?
4. What are things that used to worry you then that don't bother you at all now?
5. Did anything serious happen to you back then that felt permanently terrible but you now have a different perspective about?

Once you've finished journaling on this for a few minutes, read back over what you've written. Circle or underline at least one thing that you notice you were really stressed or struggling with five years ago that you've since long moved on from or feel really differently about.

As hard as it may seem to believe right now, the same is true for the struggle you're going through now. It is not permanent. It may take time, but you can work through it. Your five-years-from-now-self knows that, and I do, too.

Question 5: How could this situation be happening *for* me?

Are you familiar with the motivational phrases "everything happens for a reason" and "life is working out in your favor?" They're popular because no one really knows for sure why things do or don't happen to us in life. Which means *we* get to choose why things happen. Given the way you view a situation determines its impact on you, why not shift from thinking life is happening *to* you to instead believing that life is happening *for* you? That latter perspective creates far more strength and inspiration than feeling like the world is constantly out to get you. There's zero upside to viewing the world through such a pessimistic lens because our thoughts prove themselves true in our lives.

If you want a better experience of the world, practice prompting your mind to view it through the lens of "How could this situation be happening *for* me?" Even if it seems unrealistic at first, just take a guess!

Here are some examples of this perspective in practice: Perhaps you missed out on a promotion because there's another job opportunity coming that you wouldn't be able to apply for if you took the promotion. Maybe you've been given a diagnosis because the world needs you to become its next advocate for research funding. As hard as your divorce has been, maybe there is another love for you out there that shows you why your first marriage never worked out.

When it comes to the future, anything is possible. The brain will naturally tell us our future in a fearful, negative light because that's its job: to think everything is out to harm us in order to keep us safe. But rather than let your caveman brain run the show, use this question to switch on your prefrontal cortex and open your mind up to the million other possibilities that could come from this struggle. We need to believe in the possibility first, because of the way confirmation bias works; if we think our difficulties are nothing more than the world robbing us of happiness, we will miss the small yet meaningful ways we could turn them into a transformative experience.

One of my younger coaching clients, Billie, is a wonderful example of this. She was devastated after her parents pulled her out of college for a year after not passing all of her classes. To be fair, she did agree to that commitment as part of them funding her tuition, but when she was faced with that reality, she was *pissed*. I let her rant about how terrible her parents were and why her whole year would be a waste. And then I asked her this deliberate question. I was first greeted by an eye roll, but I asked her to use the week before our next session to just simply be curious about the possibility of how this could all work out in her favor. She reluctantly agreed, saying "What else do I have to lose?"

A few days later her Dad suggested she join AmeriCorps, a volunteer program that does amazing work in communities around the United States. She'd never considered it before, and she wasn't sure if she'd get in or if she'd like it, but she thought it was at least worth trying. A few weeks later, she got her acceptance letter and set off for what she now describes as "an adventure of a lifetime." She ended up serving her country in many different ways, including being part of the COVID relief team in Salt Lake City and all hands on deck for wildfire mitigation in California. She learned a whole new range of skills, made amazing new friends and experienced things she'd otherwise never have had the chance to do. She then returned to college as a whole better version of herself who was ready to dedicate herself to her studies, and is now loving life working as a behavior therapist.

Today, if you ask Billie if she'd go back in time and change what happened, she'd say that she wouldn't change a thing. By recognizing her thoughts, reflecting on them, and choosing to *redirect* her thoughts to the possibility of how this could be an opportunity for her, Billie transformed a crappy situation into a life-changing win.

You can do the same, too. Planting the seed in your mind of how a setback or loss could be working out in your favor, is where it all begins.

*   *   *

I hope by taking you through each empowering question one by one, you now have a greater understanding of just how powerful questions can be in directing our mind to finding creative solutions and novel ways to work through our struggles and feel better about our circumstances so we can create better outcomes from them.

Using questions to redirect your mind prompts you to come up with your own thoughts and perspectives. These questions will reveal to you how much of your own wisdom you already have to better handle your own struggle or setback. They help clear up all the judgment, fear, and negativity that comes from those dead-end questions we ask ourselves. It's like on a cloudy day, the sun doesn't actually disappear from the sky; it's still shining like it always does, the clouds are just blocking its rays from getting through to the Earth. But the sun is always present; always shining; always there. I think the same is true when it comes to our own wisdom and insights. As humans, we are born with incredible capacity to be brave, resourceful, and creative, it's just that so much of our automatic negative thoughts get in the way of us accessing our most courageous selves. These empowering questions help us reconnect with that brave part of ourselves.

That's why I love this strategy so much. I don't know more about the world or life than you do; in fact, no one knows more about your life than you do, so at the end of the day only you know what is really best for you. These questions can help you find that clarity and courage, so please use them to navigate through your challenges and find resilience whenever you need to.

Here's a list of four simple steps that you can reference anytime you need to take control back over the purposeful part of your brain when it begins to spiral over a situation you can't control.

1. Open up your copy of the five deliberate questions from this chapter in your notebook or Notes app, or the worksheet downloadable by the QR code, and take time to write down answers to each of these five questions. Remember that your brain may default to "I don't know," just encourage yourself to take a guess as there's no right or wrong answers here, and we're more creative and resourceful than we often realize.

2. Take a few minutes to reflect on each answer you've written. Circle and highlight one or two perspectives you've written down that feel most helpful or empowering.

3. Rewrite the most helpful and empowering thoughts somewhere you can see them daily. If you're a digital person, set the empowering thought as a daily reminder on your phone—choosing a time for the reminder to go off that you know is particularly challenging for you (e.g. setting the empowering reminder right before a meeting, if you usually get overwhelmed or intimidated in speaking to the executives). You may also like to get creative and set the empowering thought as the background on your phone using a site like Canva to help you design it. If you're more old-school, like me, and prefer pen and paper, write the empowering thought onto a sticky note and put it wherever you feel will be most helpful to see it, whether that's on your mirror, at your desk, or even in your wallet. Just make sure whatever format you choose, your reminder is somewhere obvious and easy for you to look at often! Remember,

your brain changes through repetition. We can't just immediately ingrain a thought into your brain, but we can train it by continually reinforcing and reminding ourselves of it.

4. If you have a thought that you like but can't quite believe it's true yet, put the words "It's possible" in front of the thought, like we discussed in Chapter 4 when we were learning how to Recognize how our thoughts made us feel. Once a day, set a reminder to write down one reason or one piece of evidence from your day why this thought could be true. For example, if you're trying to believe that "It's possible that my next opportunity is on its way and little by little I'll earn it," after not getting that promotion, you could be writing down proof from your week like, "I received a compliment from my boss today," or "I gained a new client this week," or "I heard another colleague was initially overlooked for promotion, and now she's on the leadership team." Looking for daily evidence in our lives and out in the world as to how our new perspective could be true is how we train our mind to believe new things and reinforce those neural pathways. Little by little, the resistance to new thoughts fades away, and you harness the power of confirmation bias to work for beliefs you *want* to believe on purpose (not the automatic ones the caveman in your brain is feeding you).

I'm hoping that this strategy has helped you uncover your own empowering thoughts to fuel resilience, but don't fear if not, this is just the beginning! The following pages are filled with even more impactful thoughts and strategies you can use to become a better CEO of your own brain and more resilient through the hardest times in life.

Purposeful Thinking

Shortly after Nicole died, her boyfriend and I were sitting in Nicole's room. He told me how they'd planned on getting engaged and what their wedding plans were going to be. He said, "She wanted you to be her only bridesmaid." It felt like my heart was ripped from my chest. I sobbed into his shoulder, feeling so touched by that honor and so broken that it would never happen.

The mainstream advice we're typically given when we're going through a rocky patch in life is to look for the positives. Although well intended, that advice is sometimes as helpful as giving someone a hammer when they're trying to paint a wall. That's not the right tool for the job, just like searching for positives isn't always the best strategy. When we're in the thick of something really painful and challenging, it can be pretty darn hard to find the good in it. In fact, sometimes there really isn't anything positive on the surface of what's happening.

When I was sitting there sobbing that I would never experience the joy of being my sister's bridesmaid and that instead, I had to face the daunting task of choosing her funeral dress, I did not feel anything positive about that. The reality is that some situations are just outright hard and unfair. Yet when we hear that there "should" be something positive in everything, and we can't find it, we can end up feeling even more frustrated and helpless. It can seem like we've been shortchanged by the world because we've missed out on the "positive thing." That's why trying to jump to the positives to feel better isn't always a useful strategy; it can backfire on us and make us feel worse.

I'm all for positive thinking in the appropriate circumstances. But when you're trying to use it to outrun your human experience and not process through the reality you've been hit with, positive thinking is not going to help you. Or even feel possible. There is no scenario in which I can imagine trying to tell myself the upside of picking out my sister's funeral dress or the fact she's been robbed of the next fifty years of her life. There's no upside to that, nor do I want to try and find one. You don't have to force yourself into seeing the good in everything. In fact, I've found sometimes accepting that perhaps there isn't any good in the situation itself is far more helpful. It helps reduce the frustration that comes from thinking you're owed more, and feeling less resentful about what you think "should be" can give you more energy to deal with "what is."

So, if trying to focus on the positives isn't always the best choice, what do I suggest you do instead?

Focus on your problems. Yes that's right, I just told you to go find problems to focus on when you're struggling. Before you think I've lost the plot, let me explain the power of problems to fuel your resilience.

The feeling that's the hardest to handle when we're trying to cope through a setback or loss is the feeling of helplessness. It's the feeling that's easiest to spiral us out of control or turn into bitterness and make us think, "What is even the point of trying? There's nothing I can do to change what I'm going through." In moments where we feel like there's nothing we can do, helplessness hits deep. And it's when we're in that frantic and helpless place that it's easy to feel like we're drowning. If we can somehow turn the helplessness into purposefulness, you're able to somewhat keep your head above water. You may still struggle, get tired, or get stressed, but there's an energy that fuels you. You find that grit in you to still get your feet on the ground and face the day. And ironically enough, it's often problems that "spark" that sense of purpose for us. Because within every problem, there is the potential for you to create something good so that your struggle or loss does not leave you empty-handed. As that's what truly fires human resilience—a reason to keep going. This doesn't come from positive thinking but rather *purposeful* thinking. This is thinking that helps you see that there is a reason that you're going through this experience. By not just looking for the silver lining, but using your two hands to create it yourself.

Even in the most extreme circumstances, we can see how this is true. Viktor Frankl spoke of how inmates would walk around comforting others and giving away their last piece of bread. They didn't try to find the "positive" in the death camps. That's impossible. But looking for the problems, seeing the misery of their fellow inmates, and wanting to solve it is what gave them purpose. It's why they could keep getting up each day despite the horrors all around them. And in doing so, they took back their power from the Nazis. Yes, they were still imprisoned. Yes, they didn't know how much longer they'd live, or if they'd even survive. But they stopped being helpless and started being powerful the second they decided, "Well, I can't change my circumstances, but there is one thing I can do today. I can save a piece of bread for my friend."

Search for something meaningful to do with your pain and struggle that contributes to something greater than yourself.

So if you're looking to spark some resilience in yourself, some reason to keep going, to keep getting up on the days when your heart is heavy or your mind is weary, stop trying to slog yourself into being positive and instead think about being purposeful. Search for something meaningful to do with your pain and struggle that contributes to something greater than yourself. That is what helps turn bitter into better and helps *you* become the good thing that happens to your circumstance.

It all starts with using the power of deliberate questions that we learned about last chapter: "What's a problem I can help solve to create purpose in my struggle?"

Maybe you've bombed your last three job interviews because you were so overly stressed and anxious, and that serves as a wakeup call to prioritize your mental health and finally call that therapist your friend recommended. Perhaps your mother is losing her hair in chemo treatment so her head gets cold all the time. It breaks your heart to see what she's going through, but rather than trying to feel good about that, you can use it as inspiration to start knitting hats for a cancer charity. Or maybe your younger brother was in an accident that left him in a wheelchair, and you realize that his favorite local café by a pond is inaccessible by wheelchair because of the flight of stairs leading down to it. So you lobby your local government to put in a ramp beside the steps and to install a wheelchair-friendly path so he and other disabled customers can still enjoy the pond and café.

Or like Nate and I did right before I left the United States in February 2020 when we were sad about being forced apart for months on end. I still remember fighting back the tears as he was driving me to the Newark airport after having just spent three amazing months together in the United States. I had to go back to Australia right as the COVID outbreak started hitting the news. There was a lot of angst between us, and Nate was kindly trying to cheer me up with loving words about how it'll pass quickly and how I'd be back in no time.

But I wasn't in a place to really believe that yet. Everything felt so uncertain, and I couldn't wrap my mind around cheery thoughts. I hated that FaceTime calls replaced hugs and snuggles together. I hated having to work around the sixteen-hour time difference and be saying good morning to him right before I was falling asleep at night. I was beginning to feel that sense of helplessness overwhelm me, so as the gray smokestacks and bleak industrial area surrounding the Newark airport whirled past my eyes, I asked myself, "What can we do to solve the problem of feeling disconnected while so far apart and help other couples who are also going through this?" That's when I turned to Nate and said, "Hey, what do you think of starting a podcast together?" I still remember the way his grin crept across his face, and we spent the rest of the car ride excitedly discussing ideas for topics we'd want to talk about on the show around relationships and sharing our experiences of navigating long distance love to support other couples struggling with it. After bouncing around a few ideas for the name of the show, we landed on "Train Wreck Your Life" in tribute to what our journey had felt like so far as we tried to figure out how to be together as a couple. As Nate's car pulled up to the curbside of the airport, although my eyes stung with tears, I also had a new sense of purpose to focus on for the plane ride home and the following months apart. I knew we'd still miss each other like crazy and there were for sure going to be some teary FaceTimes (there were plenty!), but I loved knowing we had something to bond over and work on *together*. That good thing wasn't just handed over to us by our circumstances, we created it by looking for the problem long distance created for us and what we could contribute to help solve for it. That's what truly ends the helplessness that sucks away our resilience—when we can find a way to do something meaningful with our pain and struggle that contributes to something greater than ourselves.

You can do the same at any moment, with whatever it is you're trying to find your way through. Just ask: What problem can I help solve to create purpose in this struggle?

Be prepared that when you ask this question for the first time, your brain may initially say "I don't know." Like we talked about in Chapter 9, its desire to conserve energy means thinking outside the box isn't it's favorite thing to do. But your brain also hates having an open loop in its circuitry, so if you keep asking yourself a question over and over enough, it will go find answers and solutions for you to close the gap. So don't expect instant answers, but I promise you in the long run, it's worth it when you experience what it's like to create your own purpose in your struggles and become the good thing that happens to your circumstance!

Given it can take some time to discover where your gifts, abilities, dedication, and focus intersect with a problem you can help solve, I'm going to give you this thirty day challenge to complete. Every day for the next thirty days, I want you to brainstorm one problem in your situation that you can help solve to create a seed of good and a greater sense of purpose. There are no right or wrong ideas here. Don't get caught up about whether your idea feels possible or realistic yet. Let your brain think big and get creative. Chat with friends or family to see if they have any suggestions. Or Google stories of other people who are going through or have been through similar things to your challenge and see what inspiration you can take from them as to what you can create from your experience.

In fact, it was this kind of thinking that changed my life forever. It was one month after Nicole's death, and I was sitting at the end of the dinner table with my laptop. I'd finished checking emails when I got curious to look into whether Nicole's accident was just an unlucky mistake or if it was something that happened often? When I Googled "Aussies on motorbikes in SE Asia," I instantly saw the alarming statistic that an Australian tourist was dying in Thailand every three days. That has gotten even worse as time has gone by—as of 2023, an Australian dies in Thailand every day. I also found you're 6.5 times more likely to die in a road accident in South East Asia than you are in Australia. Plus, Thai roads have been ranked among the top two deadliest roads in the world.

My stomach dropped. If my sister had known those alarming stats, she never would've gotten on that bike, as she was not a risk-taker by any means. It's just so easy to get complacent when you're overseas and do as the locals do. We also tend to think that bad things like accidents happen to other people, right? Not us or our family. I think we can all admit we've fallen for that invincibility mindset before, especially when we were younger. A few scrolls later, and I came across a video on YouTube of a drunk young Aussie tourist on a bike in Bali—his helmet was barely on, and he was screaming and cussing at the reporter, thinking it was hilarious.

And so did the comments. Most of them said something like, "funniest interview ever—I've watched it 20 times and I can't stop laughing!" My blood began to boil. It was November 20, 2012, one month to the day since Nicole died, and here were these idiots laughing their heads off about being reckless on a bike in the same part of the world my sister was killed in an instant. I bet they wouldn't have thought having to choose flowers to sit on her coffin was hilarious. I immediately wanted to throw my laptop against the wall and scream. But then I reflected on how that just leads to yet another problem. Instead I paused, recognized my anger was coming from the fact that I was assuming the man in the video didn't care, and reflected on how that anger made me act in a careless way myself. But what if I reframed this guy's recklessness as coming from ignorance or a lack of understanding of just how deadly Thailand's roads are. That is a problem I can actually help solve. So I closed my laptop, took a deep breath and asked that question, "How can I help solve this problem of Aussies being unaware of how dangerous roads in South East Asia can be?"

Instantly a girl I had heard of, Anna Wood, flashed into my mind. She was a 14-year-old girl from Australia who died from taking an ecstasy pill at a rave—the first one she ever took, and it poisoned her quickly. Her friends were too afraid to get help so she died a slow and tragic death far too young. Her parents went around to schools sharing Anna's story to save other teens from making the same mistake. Hearing their story left a big enough impact on me that I refused to ever touch drugs. And that's what helped me realize that I could create good from my sister's death, by warning others of the dangers of riding a motorbike without a helmet, especially on unfamiliar foreign roads with loose laws and regulations. I wanted people to understand how crucial it was to be wearing a helmet—no exceptions.

So on November 20, 2012, with a fateful YouTube video, a story of another tragedy, and my own raw pain mixed with deep enduring love for Nicole, the seed of good was planted in my mind of creating a travel safety campaign that I could take to schools around Australia to try save lives in honor of Nicole. My family had already started the Nicole Fitzsimons Foundation to give grants to performers and athletes in tribute to her legacy of always encouraging people to follow their dreams. I could see the potential for another aim of the Foundation to be about travel safety and how to ensure other families didn't have to go through what my family did. I began to visualize speaking to thousands of students and sharing travel tips alongside Nicole's story with them and imagining how impactful that could be. The fact we had video footage of the accident suddenly really felt like it was for a reason. Of course it's heart wrenching to watch it, and I could throw it under the bed and never look at it again, but that still doesn't change the fact it happened. I realized I could change whether it happened to someone else through sharing that footage. Seeing such a young, bright, beautiful life like Nicole's taken before your eyes in a split second is something that is unforgettable and can help to break the sense of invincibility that often puts us in those situations in the first place. Creating a travel safety presentation for high schools felt like exactly what I was meant to do next.

There was one problem—I was straight out of university and had just taken on a full-time position with a corporation. I'd given them a two year commitment to work on the marketing team, and I felt obliged to fulfill that commitment. Deep down, I think I always knew I was never going to be fulfilled there now that my life had been thrown upside down, but I began working there in January, three months after Nicole had passed away. I was grateful for the opportunity to have a full-time job so quickly out of college, but each day I couldn't wait to get home to work more on Nicole's charity, to email schools to ask if I could speak with their students, and piece together my first PowerPoint presentation about travel safety. It didn't take me—or my boss at work—long to realize that I couldn't keep trying to do both roles at the same time. It wasn't fair on the company that had given me such a huge opportunity as a young professional to not give it my all.

But truth is, my heart wasn't in it at all. I was pursuing the corporate world because I thought I should so I could make lots of money and get the nice house and car and follow the yellow brick road to wealth and success. But one thing death teaches you is how little material things matter in the big picture of life. I had wrapped my whole identity around being a high achiever, yet I was working so hard to achieve something that I didn't really even care about.

I chose to do a business degree because my Dad and brother were in the business world and hey, wearing a pencil skirt and heels to work sounds kind of cool. Yes, I'm not kidding, that was on my list of reasons to choose working in the corporate world. I really hadn't yet found something else meaningful to put my time and energy towards. Until now.

Now I had that burning desire to take my travel safety presentation about Nicole right around Australia. I dreamed of working with the Australian Government to help Nicole's legacy make a real impact on the attitude Aussies take overseas with them. Not just in terms of risk taking, but also what you can do if you do happen to end up in strife overseas by ensuring you have proper travel insurance. I never thought I'd be twenty years old and passionate about travel insurance, but had Nicole not had that insurance, our family would've been hit with over $50,000 in medical bills, which is the last thing you want to deal with when you've just found out a family member has died. Medical bills overseas can be astronomical for foreigners because our health insurance back at home doesn't cover us in foreign countries. Yet no one really explains this to us, and travel insurance is typically the last thing on our minds because no one wants to think of bad things happening on vacations. Yet the reality is, it does. Unfortunately far too often. So learning about the value of travel insurance is another lesson I scooped up from my sister's accident and realized I could turn into a powerful message for others to benefit from for their travels, too.

So I had the message, the voice, and the drive, but not the freedom to do it. I was still technically an employee of the company, and I had to make the choice: do I stay at the job that gives me the security of a paycheck and a stable path forward at the company, or do I take a leap of faith and throw myself into pursuing a dream that wasn't just unknown, there was no path. I'd have to build it myself and figure out how to get the attention of schools and be given time with their students so I could share this presentation with them. Oh, not to mention this path was going to be unpaid for the foreseeable future. It didn't make any sense to do it from a logical standpoint. But from a healing and resilience perspective, it was everything my heart needed to do. I needed to create something good from my sister's death in order to be able to come to a place of peace with it. I needed to ensure her legacy had a positive impact, just as she always had done throughout her life. I needed to find a sense of purpose, and this was it for me. So when I got a phone call from a family member who tried convincing me that leaving my corporate job to take on Nicole's charity full time was short sighted and I was just lost in my grief, I thanked them for their concern and then opened up my laptop. This time, I began crafting my resignation letter to my boss.

If I'd just waited for life to hand me the good in my sister's death, I'd still be waiting. I'd still be bitter. I'd still be helpless. Although my sister's death and your personal struggle could be entirely different, they're also very much the same. They're life hitting us with the unexpected. As it's going to, because that's life. Everything that happens next—who you become, the people you meet, what you learn, how you grow, where it leads you—is entirely up to you. Your response-ability dictates what comes next. No one can take that power from you. The pursuit of travel safety awareness hasn't stopped my struggle—I still struggle without my sister and miss getting to chat to her every day—but it's made my struggle purposeful. It's given my life and Nicole's death meaning.

As self-help author Napoleon Hill once said, "Every adversity, every failure, every heartache carries with it the seed of an equal or greater benefit." The keyword here is *seed*: the good in what you're going through might not be on the surface, but if you look for the problems surrounding it and how you could create good from it, you can not only uncover that seed of good but help grow and nurture it into something more. Something that is so purposeful that even if you still wish things hadn't happened the way they did, by being purpose driven and realizing the responsibility to build meaning into this experience is up to you, you get all of your power back. You don't let your circumstances get the final say. You find your reason to keep pushing on, simply by continually redirecting your mind to "What problem can I solve to help create purpose in this?"

And yes, coming up with solutions and ideas for this is going to demand the next level of your creativity, courage, and problem-solving skills, but that's the point, because as a human being you have been designed on purpose to grow through adversity, adapt to change, and solve problems that initially seem insurmountable. I mean, think of how much you've already grown and overcome over the last five years. You were built for these struggles and these struggles were built for you to be able to contribute, connect, and to be there for others with more depth and understanding. But it doesn't happen by chance, only by choice—the choice to take responsibility for your response-ability. To shift from passively expecting the world to just hand you the positive, to actively being the creator of it. To look for problems that hold the potential for you to be part of the change that you want to see in the world.

Life won't always give you the good in adversity, but it will always give you the raw materials to create it.

Life won't always give you the good in adversity, but it will always give you the raw materials to create it. Recognize, reflect, and redirect your mind again, again, and again. Never surrender your power. You can't control what happened. But your response really is your choice.

11

Value Your Values

In past chapters, we've talked about the ways that we can become more resilient by creating a sense of purpose out of the losses we face. Without cultivating purpose, your strength to persevere will fade quicker than a sunset in the dead of winter. However, it's not just when we're going through rough times that feeling a sense of purpose is important; it's also crucial to our overall well-being in life. Unfortunately, in a world that's becoming increasingly driven by what we see online, too many of us get swept away pursuing what we think we *should* want, not what we actually want. And believe it or not, it's when life gets turned upside down or you're blindsided by a setback that you're given a good chance to reflect and reassess your core values—what beliefs, principles, and personal qualities matter the most to you—and whether you're really living those values. Because if you're not, you risk feeling a discontentment that tends to permeate through all areas of your life. You may have worked your butt off to get the money, the job title, the house, the amazing girlfriend, yet something still feels missing. That's because your core values are your internal moral compass, and if you're not living in alignment with them, there's no amount of external success that can fill that void. Yet, too many of us are blindly chasing goals and reacting to life without understanding what we really want to stand for and what qualities matter most to us. Whether it's kindness, bravery, freedom, creativity, or open mindedness, clarifying your core values is one of the most important gifts you can give to yourself and your capacity for resilience.

The first step is to get clear on what your core values actually are. Growing up, many people asked me, "What are your goals? What do you want to achieve?" However, very few people ever asked me, "What are your values? Who do you want to *be* in the world?" So it's no wonder I stressed about the outcome of my actions, became hyperfocused on getting validation from my achievements, and sought praise and external success, like getting a good corporate job, because it seemed to be the only thing that mattered to people.

Then one day I realized, it didn't. Writing my sister's funeral speech taught me that if you can count something by a number— like the amount of money in your bank account, your weight, your grades—it doesn't matter that much at the end of your life. How your life feels is so much more important than how it looks. If you've got an Ivy League degree hanging on the wall for a career that you've never had much interest in other than to try to make your father proud, your wall may look full, but your heart might feel empty.

I can relate to that feeling that way before I did this work on clarifying that my core values are courage, kindness, freedom, curiosity, determination. We all get bombarded with so many suggestions and ideas on everything you should and shouldn't do with your time, money, career, fashion, choices in friends and relationships, it's so easy to lose yourself to the storm of opinions and ideas around you. But just like a ship lost at sea uses a lighthouse to safely navigate through stormy waters and stay on track to your destination, your life values can help you navigate through turbulent times with

Your life values can help you navigate through turbulent times with more character and courage.

more character and courage, and ensure you're moving toward what matters most to you and who you actually want to be before the world told you who you should be. Once you know your core values, it becomes much easier to recognize ways you can build meaning into your hardships.

When you recognize that your mind is spinning over all the loss and bad things about your situation, simply redirect your mind to this deliberate question: "Which of my core values does this give me the chance to practice?" This question immediately helps you reframe the situation into an opportunity for *you* to be the good thing that happens to your situation. To think about what opportunity the situation gives you to become more of the person you want to be.

This strategy is incredibly helpful in overcoming the resentment that's easy to feel toward life for being so hard and unfair. Especially when it feels like you've done everything you can and things still don't work out. Maybe you didn't go on a vacation with friends so you could prep for a big pitch your company was pushing for, but the client didn't give you a second glance. Maybe you never drink and drive, yet the person who t-boned your car and killed your best friend, went and did exactly that. Some things never make sense or will never be reconciled as fair. And so when we ask ourselves, "Why is this happening?" it seems like the only answer is because we're unlucky or the world is out to get us. And on top of that resentment, some things in life can be outright scary—like going in for your first round of chemo, going on your first date after your divorce, or walking into your boss's office to hand in your resignation. Some challenges can tempt us to hate on the world, others can make us fear it, and both of these things come from thinking that these difficulties rob us of the life experience we were "meant" to have.

You could choose to view adversity as something that takes away from your fulfillment in life and only causes you to suffer more, but that will make you feel more miserable. Having an adversarial relationship with the world makes it hard to feel strong when you think it's all rigged against you. However, asking, "Which of my core values does this give me the chance to practice?" is a way to view your life that will help you feel much less helpless and far more empowered to handle whatever it throws your way. It helps reduce fear and frustration, and puts our focus back on what we can control: ourselves—who we are and what we can contribute to the situation to create something from our loss.

In fact, in *Man's Search for Meaning*, Viktor Frankl wrote about how we need to stop focusing so much on what we expect life to give us and shift our focus more to "what life expected from us." Reflect on your relationship with your life for a moment: do you expect it to always give you what you want? On the surface, we may want to answer "No, of course not," but truthfully, when we feel frustrated or resentful for things not going to plan, it means we had an expectation that it "should have" gone our way.

Our relationship with life needs to be like every other healthy relationship: a two-way street. By that I mean, sometimes we will be able to find the good in our adversity. Other times, it's up to us to *create* it. Either way, there's no struggle without purpose as long as we own that sometimes it's on us to create the good through either solving problems or living our values. In an unfair world, a relationship of giving and taking, finding and creating, sounds quite fair to me. Stepping into this outlook not only builds your resilience but improves your relationship with life. We can become a creator of the good when we dig into the good that's in us and connect our struggles with our core values and how we can bring them to the situation.

Rather than believing life is just out to get you, by seeing the ways in which your difficulties are giving you the chance to live your values and grow your character, you'll find yourself letting go of resentment and self-pity and gaining so much more resilience to actually get through the hard thing. Remember: resilience can only be built during difficult times. With no pressure or challenges pushing up against you, it's not possible to practice resilience.

Take a basketball player, for example, who wants to prove what he's capable of to his team. The coach gives him the opportunity to take the penalty shot with three seconds left on the clock while they're one point behind on the scoreboard of the championship game. It's a very high-pressure moment, but it's not like the player gets mad at the coach about asking him to do it. In fact, he's excited by it. He realizes the opportunity he's been given, not in spite of the pressure but because of it. It's easy to shoot hoops in practice, but to really step into his greatness there needs to be this pressure and challenge in the moment.

The same can be said for your daily challenges—they're not in your way to creating a fulfilling life; they are a necessary part of it, because a meaningful life is a value-driven life. Tragedies and setbacks really are your biggest opportunities to walk the walk and respond to your life from your values (rather than your automatic thoughts and fears), experiencing that priceless sense of fulfillment when you do.

A client of mine, Valentina, was in tears after being diagnosed with celiac disease only a week after her beloved cat passed away and she was laid off from her job. Her heart was on the floor, and I could see a weariness weighing heavy on her shoulders. "I just don't know how much more I can take. So many changes at once. It's not fair." I completely empathized with her. I didn't want to rush her through the natural human emotions she needed to feel to process the losses coming her way.

Instead, I asked Valentina to grab her journal and look at how she could live each one of her core values in response to these losses. When she did this, I felt her demeanor lift a little. She suddenly had something to focus on that was in her control—the character she brought to these circumstances and the kind of person she wanted to be. Suddenly, celiac disease wasn't a killjoy to all the foods she loved to eat, but a chance to practice her value of open mindedness and try new foods until she found some gluten-free snacks she enjoyed. Losing her cat was a chance to live her core value of love and connect the sadness she was feeling to the gratefulness for having had that cat in her life for eleven beautiful years. As for being laid off, Valentina realized this was her "courage" moment; she had chosen courage as a core value yet admitted she'd played it safe for almost all of her adult life. She'd talk herself out of pursuing teaching and went for a degree in finance instead, thinking a big paycheck would be worth giving up her dream. She'd been bored senseless living in a world of spreadsheets and had secretly wanted to give her love of teaching another chance. But every time she was on the verge of quitting, she clung to the certainty of a secure paycheck and comfort of the familiar. Now that was being pulled from beneath her feet, was she going to stay clinging to the certainty of a job (which turns out, wasn't so certain after all!) or step into courage and living a value that means so much to her?

These are the valuable questions we want to ask ourselves when life gets tough—not resenting the world for it happening, but being curious about where we can step into our values to find healing or ways forward that help us grow into who we really want to be.

Because here's the thing, when life is easy and things are going our way is when it's easiest to lose sight of our values. To get hooked on the external praise or get complacent in our character. I remember far too many times getting snappy with my sister because I was too stressed about work or obsessing over an outfit in the mirror, wanting it to be perfect so others would give me attention. Easy living is often shallow living. But anytime there's resistance or pushback from life where it gives us an unwanted circumstance to deal with, that's actually when some of the best qualities of humanity—like perseverance, curiosity, courage, kindness, compassion—can shine through. It's like the good old cliche, "You need darkness for stars to shine." Well, the same goes with our values and character. Adversity is our greatest opportunity to not just say that you value courage or generosity, it's our greatest chance to actually live it. Doing this will never leave you empty-handed; every time you step up and focus on living your values in a tough situation, you will grow your character, resilience, and confidence. With that newfound confidence, your life can open up in a very big way because you're no longer seeing setbacks as something to be feared but something to be embraced as an opportunity to grow.

From burying my sister at a young age, I learned that your legacy, or the impact you have on those around you, doesn't come from your accomplishments, titles, or awards. It is how you handle your failures along the way. It's your character and your values. How you treat people, how you react to adversity, how you love. It's not something you just whip up when you're eighty, it's something you're writing into the hearts of those around you every single day.

So now I've explained the value of knowing your values, it's time to get to know your own values! Start a new page in your Notes app or notebook and title it "My Core Values." Or download the accompanying journal page for this activity by scanning the QR code. Start by answering the following prompts.

1. Thinking about people you find inspiring can help you better understand what qualities mean the most to you. Write down the names of three people you admire or who inspire you. They can be people you personally know, celebrities, or characters from movies, shows, or books. Then next to their name,  briefly write why you've chosen them. What is about them that inspires you the most? What is it about their character or way of being that you'd like to be more like in your life?

2. Reflecting upon what you want your legacy to be in the world helps zoom you out of the heaviness of now to see the big picture of the character and qualities you really want to live true to most in life. Finish the prompt: I want to be remembered in life as the person who . . .

3. Think of your best self, aka the person you want to be. How do they handle challenges? What character do they show? What qualities do they bring to their relationships?

4. Reflect on different areas of life that you've been feeling restless or discontented with lately. Why have you been feeling that way? Is there a value or need that isn't being met? For example, is your job lacking creativity? Is your relationship not spontaneous enough? Or are you feeling worn out from constantly criticizing yourself? What feels like it's been missing from your life?

5. Reflect on areas which feel most fulfilling or meaningful to you lately. What are things you do that fill up your cup and make you feel most alive? Why? What need or value is being fulfilled there?

Once you've taken time journaling to these prompts, read through your answers. Then, find the Values List in the Appendix at the end of the book. Take some time to read through the list and, using your answers from the journaling prompts, write down ten core values that matter most to you. Compare them with your answers from the prompts to see which values overlap the most with the qualities and characteristics you journaled about. These become your top *five core values*.

We really want to clarify the five core values that you think matter above all else when it comes to qualities and characteristics you want to bring to life. The other five values you selected are still part of your values, but if you try to focus on more than five core values, it is typically hard to remember them all, which dilutes the power of core values in the first place.

If it's hard to pick five out of the ten great values you picked, you could try noticing the ones that are really similar to each other. For example, love and kindness are technically different, but at the same time they're close enough to each other that I suggest blending one into the other and picking the word you really resonate with most as your core value.

After you've done the work on clarifying your top five core values, we want to connect them back to the situations you're struggling with in your life so we can begin to see where the opportunities lie to live true to your values and create more meaning in your experience.

In your journal or Notes app, list all the different things that are feeling hard to deal with in life right now. You may list one thing or twenty things, and that's okay. Just get these situations out in front of you; then we can take each one individually. Next, answer this question:

"How is this situation giving me the opportunity to practice each one of my core values?"

Now again, the instinct of our brain may be to say, "It's not." But I promise you that isn't true. Every situation—no matter how big or small—is a chance for us to live our values and feel more fulfillment on the other side.

Let me show it to you in practice, using the situation I faced when I first moved to New Jersey in 2020 and Nate was traveling a lot in the military. He'd just got home after a couple of weeks away, and said to me, "Honey, I'm home for a full two weeks now, let's make the most of it together." I was so excited and remember going through our gym workout planning out in my head some fun dates I wanted to go on together while he was home.

I'll never forget the look on his face when he walked up to me while I was on the shoulder press machine and said, "I have to go straight home now and pack my bags, work has called me out on another trip." A lump formed instantly in my throat while I tried to fight back the tears that were welling in my eyes. I knew it wasn't his fault, and I couldn't be mad at him for serving his country—it was a noble thing he was doing, which made my emotions harder to process. I didn't know where to place my pain.

I tried to do my default "bottle it all up" reaction, but I knew I couldn't keep doing that. I was beginning to badly struggle with loneliness and going back to Australia was not something I wanted to do (in fact, it wasn't even an option as the borders were still closed), so I knew something had to change. I was still doing my daily walks, workouts, and coaching. But in-person events were still banned, so I was missing getting to speak, plus I was thousands of miles away from my family and friends. I tried to make small talk with people in my housing community but it was still at a time when people would step back from you on sidewalks and want distance from strangers. Many also spoke a different language and had young kids and families. I just really couldn't find someone to connect with.

My dog, Jaku, became my main source of comfort and connection. And although the beauty of chatting to a dog is they don't judge or repeat whatever craziness you share with them, I was really missing hanging out with a girlfriend and having a good meaningful chat over a glass of wine. My levels of serotonin—the chemical you get from bonding and socializing with others—was seriously low, and my mental health felt way out of balance. So after Nate left and I'd soaked my pillow with tears, I grabbed my notebook and began to journal about this exact question: How can I live my core values in this situation? What does that look like?

So how does Nate being whisked off on another trip after being away for four weeks straight, give me a chance to live my values of courage, kindness, freedom, curiosity, determination? Here's what I wrote.

- **Courage**—*Take Nate up on his suggestion to call his sister, who also had a husband in the military and could understand how tough things like this can be.* (We hadn't had a chance to get to know each other much yet so the idea of being so vulnerable with her made me nervous—which is why I connected it with courage). *I can also call my Dad and cry.* (Again, I'm not normally very vulnerable with my Dad, and I hadn't wanted to worry my parents, but a good cry with a parent can be good for the soul!) *Ask the one friend I had made in the apartment complex to go for coffee and a walk with me. Reach out to friends back home to organize more FaceTime calls and be real with them about how I'm feeling.*
- **Kindness**—*Not judge my feelings and allow myself time to feel my way through them. Take myself to get my lashes done. Keep going for my daily walks and workouts. Don't overschedule coaching calls. Acknowledge myself in the mirror each day and say, "I'm proud of you—keep going."*
- **Freedom**—*This one is tough, as freedom is something I feel I really don't have right now and it feels crippling. I can't go back to my home country, I can't go out and speak to audiences, I can't spend time with my husband. But come on brain, come*

up with one way I can practice freedom . . . Jump in the car with Jaku and go for a long walk along the river across the bridge. I always walk around the apartment walking trail, but this is one way I can remind myself I'm still free to roam around many places with Jaku even if Nate isn't here. Also, Viktor Frankl speaks of the freedom we can find within our own mind and what we choose to focus on, and I can choose to keep focusing on how it will feel to finally walk down the aisle to Nate on our wedding day and say "I do" together. Oh, and I also have the freedom to watch all the girlie shows on Netflix without any complaints from Nate!

- **Curiosity**—*I wonder . . . that's what curiosity is all about. Being open minded about what could be rather than making assumptions, so I wonder how this is going to serve our relationship in the big picture? I wonder how this will make us stronger? Long distance from Australia to the United States made us better communicators and taught us how to love from afar, so perhaps this is another one of those growth-worthy moments for us.*

- **Determination**—*Determination is only something you can practice when the going gets tough and there are resistance or challenges holding you back from what you want, so if I didn't have this challenge of being apart from Nate so much, I wouldn't be able to practice being determined in my love for him. Many people say, "I'd move mountains for you," but the fact we're not really quitting on each other during this difficult time shows our level of commitment to each other, which is a beautiful thing. My "why", my reason to keep persevering through this time apart is because the pain of ending this relationship would be far worse than the temporary struggle I am feeling now. The joy Nate brings to my life far outweighs the sadness of certain circumstances. This is worth it.*

So, there you go. There's my heart and my struggle on a page for you all to see. Outside of losing my sister, that eight-month period when Nate was traveling a lot and I was in a new foreign country trying to set up my business on my own, was one of the hardest periods of my life. But I choose not to resent it because I can see how it's helped me grow into my values even more and stretch my capacity to be resilient.

Now I want you to practice doing the same. Find your notebook or pull up your Notes app and get writing! List each core value and then just start brainstorming any ideas you can come up with, big or small, like you can see in my example. Get creative and stretch your imagination, and be playful with it if you need to. Just find at least *one* thing for every value. I promise you it's always possible.

Here's another example.

Say you're struggling because your ex cheated on you. This could give you the opportunity to practice your value of bravery by:

- Signing up to therapy for the first time
- Deleting your ex's number rather than ruminating on why he did it
- Go speed dating with a friend even though you're still scared of getting hurt again.

Or maybe after receiving a rejection email from the job you were so excited about gives you the chance to live your value of open mindedness by:

- Reminding yourself this could be working out for the best
- Ask for feedback on why you weren't selected so you can learn from it before you apply for the next one

- Find three other jobs to apply to within the next week—who knows what else could be out there!

Or your father's diagnosis with terminal cancer lets you practice your value of kindness by:

- Making the effort to ring him twice a week (rather than telling yourself "I'm too busy")
- Calling your sibling weekly and making sure they're doing okay, too
- Not working overtime so you can spend more time with your kids
- Making sure you come back during the holidays this year because you've been reminded that we don't have forever with loved ones.

These are just some examples to get your own creative juices flowing as to how you can reframe your difficulties into opportunities to live your values.

I love this values question so much, because it's not forcing you to try and feel positive about the situation, but it does help you focus on things you can control and contribute, which is such a powerful source of resilience. It redirect us from this passive place of "What can I get from this situation?" to a proactive place of "What can I give to it?" To live our values and to reframe challenges as our greatest opportunity to do so is a choice that we each get to make every minute of every day. In the next chapter I will introduce you to a daily practice that helps our ability to do this and find creative ways to "be the good" in the bad stuff life throws our way.

To live our values and to reframe challenges as our greatest opportunity to do so is a choice that we each get to make every minute of every day.

12

One Good Thing

If you look up the hashtag #grateful on Instagram, you'll find more than 57 million posts. Gurus and mental health experts around the world promote the power of gratitude to get you through tough times. One thing missing from many of the #grateful posts is an explanation of the science behind *why* it works and what it actually takes to make gratitude have a positive impact on your life. In fact, I think gratitude, appreciating what you have and expressing thanks for it, is becoming more of a buzzword that gets thrown around than a skill people are actually practicing in their lives to support their resilience. People are quick to post up a cute photo of their dog or their favorite holiday picture with #grateful but often with the intention to show how great their lives are to others rather than actually slowly down to appreciate and soak it up for themselves.

So in this chapter, we're going to explore why, during the shittiest times in our lives, we should redirect our minds to being grateful. Then I am going to teach you my daily gratitude practice, which is similar to what you've likely heard before—but with a twist. That twist is, when life is at its worst, not only should we practice gratitude for what we're given in our life but what we *give* to life, for an all-around sense of purpose, positivity, and empowerment.

Why Be Grateful When Life Sucks?

I know it might sound counterintuitive to be grateful when you're going through some of your toughest times. But when you dig into the research behind it, it really makes sense. Just like when your windshield is frosted over on a cold winter's morning, and you need to blast it with warm air to help it defrost, purposely taking time to notice and express things to be grateful for—no matter how small—helps dissolve away the negative emotions that were clouding your vision. And I don't mean this figuratively, either. Once we're in a negative headspace, your brain will be primed to focus on more negative things.

Remember our brain biases from Chapter 5—especially our negativity bias, our brain's tendency to focus on losses and negative things, and confirmation bias, how our brain seeks evidence for our current beliefs and filters out information that contradicts its beliefs? Yes, that's what's at play here. It's like we're wearing "skepticals," a negative lens that can only take in the bad parts of our day and perpetuates our bad mood. From not being asked to join your colleagues for drinks after work to the printer malfunctioning midway through your report that's due in ten minutes, every setback or difficulty feels heightened in our brain as it hyperfocuses on just how crappy things are in that moment. Not because it's trying to make your life more difficult, but because negative thought patterns—maybe it's saying "everything sucks right now"—release stress chemicals in your brain that narrow your peripheral vision and make you lose perspective on the big picture and the other things happening around you that actually aren't so bad.

Redirecting your brain to gratitude is the fastest way for you to cut through all the toxic negativity spiraling in your brain that's making it harder for you to handle things. Because every time we purposefully look around and find something to be grateful for, serotonin and dopamine ("feel good" chemicals) get released in your brain, which helps boost your mood. Researchers Heather A. Wadlinger and Derek M. Isaacowitz found that when we feel more positive, our peripheral vision expands, and our ability to see the big picture, connect the dots, and think outside the box improves, so we open up to new perspectives about what can be gained from any experience, helping you feel inspired to take more positive action.

In the months after my sister's death, I genuinely believe gratitude was one of the only things that kept me going. Because I knew that I wasn't going to have a good day for a very long time, and that most days were going to be filled with tears, tissues, and moments of sobbing so hard I felt like I could barely even breathe. Sometimes that made it hard to want to get out of bed at all. I didn't want to live in this reality of not having my sister down the hallway anymore. But the only reality I didn't want to live with even more would be the reality of not having had Nicole in my life as my sister at all. To me, that would have been the greatest tragedy. As much as I didn't want to deal with that grief, I also looked at the fact that the only way to grieve someone is to have lost someone—someone that you loved and cared about. And the only way to lose someone you care about is to have had them in your life to begin with. They may be gone now, but they brought the gift of their love and connection into your life.

So, buried within the depths and pain of grief, there is a huge amount of gratitude to be found, because whether that person was in your life for twenty years, twenty weeks, or twenty minutes, if they've touched your heart in some special way, you will grieve their loss. I would rather be spending my life with a broken heart that grieves my sister, than a heart that was never touched by her to begin with. In fact, I've found that anyone I've met who's also lost someone very close to them and seems to be finding their way through the grief in a healthy way, all say similar things. *"Well, at least I got to have them in my life."*

Gratitude helps us keep perspective and find strength to cope with unfair realities that we wish could be different, but it also helps us see that at least it wasn't a worst case scenario. Gratitude not for the fact that my sister died, but for the fact that she lived, was the rope I hung on to tightly to stop the grief sweep me over the edge. I get to grieve my sister. I don't want to; but at the same time, I do. The universe was cruel to take her so young, but it wasn't so cruel that it didn't keep her from blessing this Earth for a brief yet beautiful amount of time. I got to be her little sister for twenty amazing years and out of all the families in the world she could've been given to, she was given to ours, and I now have the honor of getting to live out her legacy and share it with others. When I chose to focus on my sister's death that way, I found the strength to hold space for the depths of my grief and the intense physical sensations that came with it. Even just this year on the anniversary of her passing, I looked to the sky and I said, "Thank you for being my sister." My grief continues to run deep, but when I refocus on the gratitude that goes alongside it, I keep from letting that pain make me bitter.

If you lost someone who means a lot to you, I want to offer you the idea that bringing in more gratitude to support yourself through the hard and painful moments is such a gift to give yourself. It's not trying to deny your grief, it's what helps you make space for it in your life. We will always grieve the person we lost, for we will always love them. Let your love be deeper than your grief, so on the days you feel like giving up, you remember why this pain is worth it. Every day we get on this Earth is another day our loved ones didn't, so it's up to us to make the most of it.

So that is one way I practiced gratitude throughout my grief journey on a grander scale. However, there was another "redirect to gratitude" practice for more day-to-day things that really helped me stay out of complete self-pity in the very early days when collapsing into a heap on the ground sobbing was very much a part of my daily life.

This gratitude practice is one of my favorites to teach my clients. It doesn't try to gaslight you into thinking everything is wonderful or there's nothing wrong at all. That's just resisting your reality. Instead, we need to embrace what is. Historian and writer Alice Morse Earle said it most eloquently: "Not every day's a good day, but there's something good in every day."

One good thing.

There is always at least *one* good thing to be grateful for.

That's all it takes to keep your brain from spiraling completely into hopelessness or helplessness. One good thing. Actively reminding myself there's still always *one* good thing even in the worst days, whether that was watching the sunrise or cuddling with my dog. No matter how many hours I'd spent crying or feeling alone, I committed to always redirecting my brain to one good thing that helped me find the strength to hold on that day and continue to engage with life in small yet meaningful ways.

I love this One Good Thing (OGT) practice because sometimes, when it feels like one thing is piling up on top of the other or your life is rocked by a tragedy where tidal waves of grief come daily, trying to look around for five good things or trying to answer the question, "Why was today a good day?" can feel too much of a stretch. But when you acknowledge and accept that perhaps today wasn't a good day overall, but redirect your brain to find *one* good thing within your day, it feels way more manageable of a task to comprehend because it's smaller and more specific, and that's where the power of gratitude lies. In the specifics.

Too often people are pretty vague when asked what they're grateful for: they'll say things like "my family," "my friends," or "coffee." Now, that's a start—it's better than not practicing gratitude at all. But it's also so vague and general that it's hard for your brain to really experience that release of dopamine and fleeting moment of joy that can come when you dial in on what *exactly* you're grateful for from this specific day. When you a really stop and take a moment to reflect upon your day and think of a specific moment or thing that made you smile or feel good—like the little smiley face that your barista put on the froth of your coffee or how nice it was of your friend to call and check in on your drive home—you are recreating more specific memories and moments in your brain, which increases the amount of dopamine, serotonin, and overall joy you will feel from that gratitude practice.

Psychologist and neuroscientist Rick Hanson explained that our brains are like Velcro for negative events and like Teflon for positive experiences—positive moments tend to slide right off due the brain's negativity bias. It doesn't need to store away positive experiences in order to keep us safe, so it doesn't give much energy to taking in the good aspects of our days. That's why we have to actively take time to reflect and soak up the positive little joys and experiences in our day, being as specific as possible in your description to help your brain experience the good feels of that moment so it's flooded with a rush of healthy chemicals that your brain needs to be more resilient.

However, there's a part two to practicing gratitude that is a huge antidote to depression and helplessness. And that is to not just take in the good from your day, but to notice and appreciate what good *you* did that day. Often, in the middle of a crisis or tough period in life, you might struggle with a lack of purpose. Gratitude practices are more impactful when you focus on acknowledging the act of kindness or contribution you did in the world to remind yourself: your hands are not too small to make a difference. By channeling your emotion into something else greater than yourself and

Your hands are not too small to make a difference.

thinking about not just "What good can I find today?" but also "What good can I do today?" can end our sense of helplessness and increase our sense of belonging, because doing good for others releases dopamine, serotonin, and oxytocin in our brain.

Even writing down daily the smallest ways you did something positive in the world—like holding the door open for the person behind you, checking in on a friend, or calling your mother for a catch up—reinforces to yourself the power you hold to know not only how to *find* the good, but *create* the good, which gives you back a greater sense of control and pride that you're being a part of the change you want to see in the world. It helps redirect us away from dwelling on our own sorrows and helps us realize we're not the only ones struggling. Self-pity can transform into self-empowerment when we look for ways we can be the good thing that happens to someone else's day.

Never discount your act of kindness as being too small, as you don't know how much that compliment meant to your coworker or how much easier you made your friend's day when you offered to walk her dog. There is something so powerful about remembering even if you can't solve all of *your* problems or struggles today, you can do something else to help someone through theirs and to help them feel more seen and appreciated, which in turn makes it easier to see and appreciate yourself. Especially as your kindness or contribution is likely to receive an expression of gratitude or thankfulness from the person at the receiving end, which again floods us with the feel-good chemicals we need to be more resilient throughout our day. But even if the person you help doesn't express gratitude for your actions, writing down one good thing you do each day fuels self-validation and appreciation, which further support your ability to keep showing up, even on the hard days.

One of my favorite songs as a kid was Jewel's *Hands* because of the chorus. The song is about resilience, and in the chorus she acknowledges that her hands are small—but that they are her own. She finishes with "I am never broken." Even little six-year-old me was taken by the power of those lyrics. To me, she's saying that at the end of the day, it's not about the size of contribution that counts, it's the fact you can contribute. No matter how small or simple, I want you to remember as a human being, you are never helpless. You can make a difference. Even if it's not directly in your own circumstances that day, you can make a difference to someone else, which in turn will help lift up your day because humans are wired for contribution and connection. Reaching out and looking out at simple ways to "be the good" each day cuts through our sense of isolation and purposelessness when you realize even when you're hurting, grieving, scared, or have puffy red eyes that glasses can't hide, you can still be the reason someone smiles that day. At the end of the day, that really is all that matters.

About five years after Nicole died, I was at a networking event chatting with a bunch of women around my age, when someone looked at me and said, "Oh my gosh, you're Nicole's sister!" I smiled big—I loved realizing how much people still remembered my sister. But what impacted me the most was what she remembered her for. She said, "Oh, I loved competing against her in dance competitions. I was always so nervous backstage, and she'd come up to me and give me a little pep talk and remind me to relax and enjoy the thrill of being on stage. One time she even came over and helped me with the ribbons on my ballet shoes that I was struggling with. She was always so generous like that."

Of all the things my sister achieved with her life, it was moments like these where I learned more about her heart and character that inspired me the most. She wasn't just focused on being the best at her craft, but being a good human to those around her. Which I know can be tough when you feel in the dumps, but I promise you, the way to begin to dig yourself out of it is letting go of focusing on just your situation and look around to see what other situations you can give to. Even if all you can muster up is a big hug and a "thank you" to your mother for giving you her shoulder to cry on that day, you expressing that gratitude to her is within itself a gift, as thanks to that expression she then experiences a sense of purpose and appreciation. Kindness inspires gratitude, gratitude inspires kindness.

I love thinking about how we'll never know how far our acts of kindness ripple through our workplace, our town, our country, and our world. You holding the door open for someone inspires them to look back and do it for someone who may have felt invisible that day, but thanks to that thoughtfulness, they feel a little more seen, and so they comment on how good their coffee is to the barista who had a fight with her boyfriend that morning and needed something to lift her spirits. Then the barista's boost in mood helps her respond with more patience to her boss, who's stressed about when the next delivery is coming, rather than snapping back at his pettiness. This starts with a simple three-second door opening. That's all it takes.

There's a saying "hurt people hurt people," but hurt people can also help heal themselves and others when we use our own struggle as a reason to stop being so negative and start being part of the good that we feel is missing. And then ensure you validate yourself for that! Even if no one else really notices, you know you're living in alignment with your values and the kind of person you want to be, and winning over our own opinion of ourselves is half the battle. Less judging your struggle and more appreciating what you're still able to give, even when you're struggling.

GRATITUDE LIST WITH A TWIST!

Okay, so now you know why gratitude is so powerful in fueling purposeful thinking and how to deepen the benefits of being grateful, it's time to put it to practice in your life! Write "One Good Thing (OGT)" at the top of a new page in your Notes app or journal. Then, split it into two columns. Title the first column "What's OGT you found today?" and the next "What's OGT you did today?" If you prefer having a page that's already especially designed for this gratitude practice, scan the QR code—I've made one just for you to download and print out! Then set a reminder on your phone to fill out this list at a specific time every day for the next thirty days. Try doing it right before bed so you can reflect on your day, and  no matter how hard it might've been, you're finishing your day with some self-appreciation and gratitude for the good things that are ever present and within our power to create.

The cool thing is, gratitude is just one of many ways to help our brain receive mood-boosting chemicals that help us be more resilient. In the next chapter, I'll reveal more of what those habits are for a happier and healthier brain, even on the hard days!

13

Simple Ways to Create a Happier Brain

So far, we've learned a lot about mindset and perspective, because in order to build resilience, it's crucial to focus on what we can control. However, sometimes we can be in such a funk that trying to manage thoughts can feel impossible. Maybe your mood feels too low and foggy to get past all the negativity your brain is spiraling into. And then it can be tempting to judge yourself for that. Like, "Ugh! What's wrong with me? Just change your thinking—it's not that hard!" Since these mindset steps are simple in theory, but not so easy in practice, in this chapter, we'll learn practical things you can do to put yourself in a better headspace. It all starts by understanding what makes your brain happy and function well at a very basic level. That then makes it easier to understand how to use tools like purposeful thinking and practicing gratitude.

Before I introduce these new practices, I want you to understand why, even if you might not feel like doing these things initially, they're still worth doing because they'll trigger the release of happy chemicals in the brain, which will inevitably help shift your mind into a better place. There is a certain mix of neurochemicals that our brains desire in order to function at its best. These four main chemicals are dopamine, serotonin, oxytocin, and endorphins. Understanding the basics of these chemicals and the role they each play in your well-being is vital to keeping your mental health in check. If we want to help a flower grow and bloom, we need to understand how much sunlight and water it needs. The same goes for our brain; we need to understand what it specifically needs to feel mentally healthy. If you leave a sunflower in the shade for twenty hours a day, it's going to wilt. If you deprive your brain of these chemicals for too long, it'll begin to take its toll on you, especially when you're going through a rough patch in life.

In the following pages, I define each of these chemicals for you and then suggest eight activities you can do to help release these chemicals in your brain in healthy ways. The cool thing is many of the activities overlap, so you're typically getting a whole mix of feel-good chemicals from each activity! As you read through my suggestions, make a note in your notebook or Notes app which activities sound most appealing to you that you want to try next time you're feeling in a funk.

For each brain chemical, I share the activity I did during the early days of losing Nicole that I think made the biggest difference in giving my brain a healthy dose of that happy chemical and the other added benefits. Everyone's a little different in their preferences though, so before that I'll list out other options you can try out also to help ensure you're doing *something* every day that's healthy for your resilience and mindset. It doesn't have to be perfect or extreme, just small little somethings.

Dopamine

Dopamine plays a key role in motivating and rewarding pleasurable behavior. This feel-good chemical is linked with the survival part of our brain and is released as reward any time you do behavior that helps keep you alive—like drinking, eating, and procreating (remember, your brain's number one mission is survival!).

Whenever you do something that feels pleasurable, a large amount of dopamine gets released into your brain. It's why we get addicted to things like social media and junk food, because whenever you eat a tasty doughnut that you'd been craving or get a notification ding on our phone from the guy you're talking to on Tinder, your brain gets a rush of dopamine. It feels great in the moment, and your brain is motivated to want to repeat that experience to get more of that chemical.

Dopamine is something we can create for ourselves through our own actions and healthy choices. And dopamine does more than just help you feel good—it plays a crucial role in memory, sleep, learning, and movement. It can be a helpful chemical to get you through tough days if you have a healthy balance of consuming versus creating it. Consuming our dopamine is when we're receiving it from a passive activity like scrolling on social media or watching Netflix. Creating our dopamine is when we receive it after taking active action ourselves like going for a jog or finishing your to-do list. The well-being benefits of dopamine are most powerful when there's a healthy balance of consuming your dopamine from instantly-gratifying things, like watching a good TV series, and creating dopamine through your own effort and action. Below are some more suggestions to help stimulate more dopamine in your brain on days when it's feeling low.

Write down a to-do list and complete a task on it
Do a physical activity that you enjoy to get a sweat on!
Listen to music that you love
Get outside in the sunlight for at least 15 minutes
Have a cold shower or ice bath
Meditate
Have a cup of coffee
Journal

This last suggestion, journaling, was a lifeline for me after Nicole died, which is interesting because I wasn't really much of a journaler before then. Yet once she died, I can't imagine how I would've gotten through those first few months without it. I would spend hours sitting up on our family balcony, legs crossed on my chair, pen in hand and tears streaming as I let all of my pain and love unravel onto the pages of my journal. For the first time in my life, I was overwhelmed with a pain so deep and so intense, there was no way I could bottle it up or pretend I didn't have time to process it. My friends didn't always quite know what to say and my parents were struggling themselves. But then I found the pages of a journal, and suddenly I found an outlet for it all. My journal became my safe place where I could just *feel*, without anyone judging me or trying to fix my feelings. Since it was a blank and private space for me to feel things freely, it helped me begin to make sense of what I was thinking and feeling, which as you learned in Chapter 1, is a huge part of the first R: recognize. Recognizing what was running through my mind and what it was I was really feeling that day helped me connect me with myself and allow space for the tidal waves of emotions to flow through me. I think my daily journaling also helped me faster reach the Acceptance phase of what happened as I was allowing time for my mind to process it and put it into words, which helped integrate the experience more into my psyche and identity, rather than trying to resist it or numb it out.

Research backs up my experience: Studies show that journaling is helpful in expressing and regulating emotions and reducing the amount of time spent brooding over unhelpful thoughts or feelings. Journaling also offers better channels for the release of dopamine, especially when you keep it up over a period of time. So even if you don't consider yourself a journaling person or have had resistance to it in the past, I encourage you to keep an open mind and practice journaling daily for at least two weeks, even if it's just two minutes a day, and see what you notice. Plus, it's an excuse to go to Target and buy a new cute journal, and who doesn't love that? I'm going to suggest a few different styles of journaling and see which one feels most natural and helpful for you to use as part of your brain care and boosting your dopamine levels in a safe and healthy way.

Brain Dumping

An oldie but a goodie when it comes to journaling is to simply brain dump everything that's swirling around your mind. No editing or filtering. No worrying about what's the right thing to write. If it's on your mind, it goes down onto paper! Write down everything from the fact you need to buy cat food tomorrow, how worried you are about your father's surgery, or how hurt you are that you saw your ex's post online with his new girlfriend. Let *everything* come out—no matter how long or short. At first you might think you don't have that much to write about, but from my experience with brain dumping, once you get going, you *really* get going!

Getting all your thoughts and feelings out onto paper itself can be a relief. Thoughts can be slippery and sneaky, hiding in our subconscious and disappearing quickly, but by taking the time to consciously focus on what's on our mind, we can bring some of those sneaky beliefs to the surface. That's when we can begin to get a handle on them. Take a moment to read back over whatever you've written, and you'll begin to understand why you've been feeling the way you do. Once you see how much you wrote about your father's upcoming surgery, you'll understand why you're so anxious. Or maybe you noticed that you think your ex's post with his new girlfriend means he never really loved you—and now you see more clearly why you feel so hurt. Being able to connect your thoughts to your feelings—step two, Reflect, of the 3 Rs—can bring insight into your internal world that you can't quite grasp when it's rolling around your mind. As they say, you can't read a label from inside the jar. We need to get those thoughts and feelings out into a safe space to explore them and understand more about where they're coming from. That can help replace self-judgment with self-awareness and understanding, which are important parts of fostering your resilience.

Prompted Journaling

One of the more popular types of journaling is to use prompts or questions to direct where your journaling goes and what you write about. As we know, our brain will naturally dwell on negativity and losses if left to its own devices. That's why prompts like the ones below are helpful in opening up your mind to focus on new and different perspectives and areas of your life that are easier to feel good about. It can also help you reflect on your own growth and areas that need more attention and support. Journaling is a powerful practice in the Redirect stage of the 3 Rs, as using those questions shared on page 105 as journal prompts can also help you expand your perspective and discover better ways to think about your situation that fuels your strength. We've already explored the benefits of gratitude and OGT lists, which is another form of journaling you can use to help release more serotonin and dopamine. On top of these suggestions for journaling questions I've already included in Chapters 8 through 12, here are some more prompts that I like to use when feeling in a rut:

Today I am feeling . . .
What's been hard about this week? Am I making it harder
    for myself? How?
What is it I'm really needing right now? How can I give that
    to myself?

The small joys I experienced today were . . .

I can do hard things. I know this because . . .

What is one thing from my past that I'm ready to let go of? Why?

Write down a difficult situation you've been dealing with. What am I learning about myself through this situation so far?

What's different about me from one year ago? What can I do now that I couldn't do then?

When is another time I've gone through hardships in life? What did that experience teach me?

If there is a greater meaning in what I'm going through right now, I think that greater meaning could be . . .

What positive changes can I make in my life as a result of this challenging experience?

What can I be proud of myself for so far this year? What can I appreciate about my strength and resilience so far?

This journaling prompt list could go on and on! Whether it's journaling to help you heal, forgive, find acceptance, or better understand yourself, there's an endless list of journaling prompts online. Just Google the topic that you're after with the words "journaling prompts," and you'll find an abundance of prompts to inspire you through your journaling journey. Even if you're just answering one question per day for a minute or two at a time, *something* is still better than nothing. You may be surprised at what you discover once you let your pen do the talking.

Journaling to a Loved One

If you picked up this book because you lost someone whom you care for deeply, then the final journaling style I want to suggest to you is journaling to your loved one directly. I did this a lot after Nicole died. Every entry in my journal was speaking directly to Nicole herself. I would let her know how much I missed her and how much I was struggling without her. I would picture Nicole and her bright smile sitting there next to me as I wrote, and it felt as though I was having a conversation directly with her. So although there was a lot of pain coming through in my entries to her, I also know that if I really were in conversation with Nicole, I wouldn't just sit there in misery, complaining about how much pain I was in. I would also want to take time to remind her how much I love her, and how grateful I am to be her sister and for all the memories that made this grief worthwhile. So that's exactly what I did when I would journal to her; I would let all of my grief and sadness come rushing out onto the paper, but then I would always finish my journal entries to her with so much gratitude for the fact I got to have her in my life and all the life lessons she's taught me. That really helped me balance out processing through the pain of her loss but also reconnect with the love that made the loss worth enduring. Think of these journal entries as everything you wish you had said to your loved one while they were here or everything you'd say to them again if they were still here. This will not only help not only keep your connection with them alive but also help you find more strength when you practice gratitude for the impact they've had on your life than if you're just sitting there focusing on the pain you're feeling. Make space on your page for the pain *and* the love—that's how we make it through grief.

Oxytocin

Oxytocin aka the "love hormone" has earned that name because it's mainly released when we're bonding or connecting with others in a meaningful way. It has antistress effects in your brain, helping us better regulate our emotions and increasing our sense of belong-ing. Since feeling alone and isolated sucks away our ability to be resilient, doing oxytocin-inducing activities on crappy days can make a big difference. Below are some of my favorite suggestions to help give your brain a healthy dose of feeling more loved and connected:

Listening to calming music

Hang out or play with your pet

Get a massage

Write a card or text to a friend expressing how much they mean to you and why

Hug someone you care about

Yoga, whether it's doing a class or a simple video on YouTube

Watch something humorous with a friend that makes you laugh

Catch up with a friend, and put your phone away while you're at it. Active and empathetic listening helps increase your oxytocin levels.

Cook one of your favorite meals for yourself and a loved one

The suggestion to laugh and find humor with a friend often gets pushed to the side when people are going through rough times. It is easy to think because they're going through something serious that they have to be serious about everything and shouldn't make a joke because it's disrespectful. But unless you're actually laughing at someone else's struggle or misfortune, humor isn't disrespectful—it's actually part of how you respect your own strug-gle because of the healthy chemicals like oxytocin that it releases to help you cope with it. In fact, an unattributed quote I saw early on after my sister died that really helped me see this was: "Every time you find some humor in a difficult situation, you win." This isn't a metaphorical win, either. Laughter reduces the stress hormones in your body and floods you with oxytocin and dopamine, which boost your ability to handle your difficulties.

Humor has played a huge role in boosting my oxytocin levels to help my brain be more resilient, right from the very beginning of our family tragedy. We were driving away from my sister's funeral and as you can imagine our hearts were as broken as it gets. We'd just endured our worst nightmare, yet I remember leaving the cemetery together laughing. Yes that's right, laughing.

I remember the joke being about something utterly ridiculous, but I'll never forget looking around and seeing a cheeky smile on my Mum's face and hearing a small chuckle from my Dad. And I cannot tell you the way in which that moment taught me the power of humor and laughter in keeping a human soul from falling apart. It showed me that you can smile through the tears and even in the depths of grief, our humanness yearns to laugh and smile. And this understanding played a very big part of my healing since losing my sister. In the weeks after her funeral I remember watching my favorite comedy shows through red raw eyes or looking at silly photos of her that made me giggle. My heart still ached, but I was able to find a moment of relief by giving it the gift of laughter. Not laughing at my pain, but laughing with it. Laughing when it hurt and sometimes until it hurt, gave me so much strength on bad days. And still does.

So, first of all I want to remind you, it's not wrong to take a moment to have fun or be silly when you are going through some heavy times like losing a loved one or receiving a bad diagnosis. It's *how* you help yourself get through those moments with the healthy chemicals laughing releases for you. You don't have to feel sad or bad 24/7. Having a laugh with the nurse in the reception area of your mother's cancer ward doesn't mean you're happy she's there and that she's so unwell. You can be sad about that and still allow yourself moments of joy. Not as a denial of reality, but as a way to help you cope with it. Life is hard; you do not need to make it harder for yourself by taking it *all* so seriously.

So, if you're really feeling stuck in a bad head space, seek your shows, movies, reels, photos, and memes that typically make you laugh or smile. If you looked at the Discover page of my Instagram, you'd see the entire thing is filled with silly reels of golden retrievers sneakily stealing their food or poodles lying on the couch with the cheeky entitlement of a spoiled five-year-old kid. When I'm feeling low and need a quick way to lighten my mood, those silly reels never fail me. The algorithm online can be a good thing, you've just got to use it in your favor and seek out what feels good to your soul to watch, and watch more of that so it keeps sending that kind of stuff your way! I only ever choose to watch puppy reels and so now my entire search page is that, and I love it. You can do the same. Purposefully choose to only watch reels and videos that make you smile or feel warm and glowy on the inside, and little by little, the algorithm will purposefully filter them onto your feed and filter out more of the negative stuff that gets posted on there.

Now like everything, our consumption of media needs to be in moderation, but that's where having daily time limits for the apps you know you're tempted to binge on can be helpful; spending no more than two hours of screen time per day for entertainment purposes is the recommended amount by experts, so commit to that for yourself. Beyond that, we may be starting to use social media as an escape mechanism rather than a "feel better" mechanism.

Endorphins

Endorphins are a group of chemicals that cause your big sweaty smile after a morning run! Known as the brain's natural pain reliever, endorphins are released in response to your body experiencing pain or stress, which is why experiencing a rush of endorphins after a run is called a "runner's high." Low endorphin levels are linked with anxiety and depression, while a healthy level of endorphins can reduce your stress levels and boost your self-esteem.

Exercise is the primary way to release endorphins, but it's not the only way! You know that warm, fuzzy feeling you get when you help someone out? Yep, that produces endorphins, too. Here are some more suggestions on how you can boost your brain's endorphin levels to help you get to a better headspace:

Watch a comedy or funny reels on social media: laughing releases endorphins!

Volunteer for a local charity event or at a local shelter

Do a form of cardio exercise

Acupuncture

Do a random act of kindness, like pay for someone's Starbucks behind you in the drive-through

Take a hot bath

Meditate

Get some form of physical activity going, whether an exercise class or trail run

Out of this list, exercise was one of the most powerful creators of endorphins to help me better handle the pain of my grief. Two days after losing Nicole, I went to my local gym, and although there was no way I could fathom picking up weights or sprinting intervals like I typically would, I got on the treadmill and started walking at 2.5 miles per hour. My steps felt heavy, shaky, and far slower than usual, but I know that physically standing up and putting one foot in front of the other not only helped release some of those healthy chemicals in my body, but was metaphorically powerful for me and the daunting journey ahead. It was if my body was telling my mind, "Just one step at a time, that's how we can and will get through this." One step, one breath at a time.

I am so grateful I didn't just shut down entirely on any sort of physical activity at all. My mind needed my body to show up for it and remind it what I was capable of. I eventually worked my way back up to my usual routine of weights and cardio, but some days were easier than others. If you could ask my trainer, she'd tell you how some days I'd be doing pull ups or squats with tears in my eyes. It wasn't like lifting weights helped me forget my sister died, but I do know it helped me process the emotion of it. I mean if you think about it, the word itself has "motion" in "e-motion." I believe that a huge part of processing the energy and sensations that our emotions release is through motion and moving our bodies. It gives us a healthy way to channel it rather than sitting still holed up in a dark room where the intensity grows because it has nowhere to go.

So even if it's the last thing you feel like doing, I suggest doing some sort of physical activity at least three times a week, even the tough weeks. That's when the benefits of the endorphins can impact you the most. Whether it's a hike outdoors or a yoga video on You-Tube, moving your body does wonders for your brain. And that's what we really need to take care of when we're feeling low.

Serotonin

The final of your brain's four happy chemicals is serotonin. Think of this chemical as your mood stabilizer. It plays a crucial role in regulating your mood, digestion, sleep, and many other vital bodily functions. If you're low in serotonin, you have an increased chance of developing depression or anxiety. The good news is there are plenty of ways to naturally release serotonin! Here are just a few.

Get outside for least fifteen minutes a day to spend time in
   the sun and out in nature

Gratitude journaling (see Chapter 12)

Eat foods high in amino acids (protein) like salmon or tofu

Aerobic exercise like jogging, biking, light hiking, or barre
   class

Deep breathing exercises (my favorite is 4:2:5—breathe in for
   four, hold for two, exhale for five)

Get a massage

Get a good night's sleep

Call a friend for a meaningful chat

The first suggestion, spending time outdoors in nature, has been
hugely therapeutic for healing my grief. Especially watching Nicole's
favorite time of day, sunrises. I would purposely wake up early and
take my heavy heart to the bay near my home and watch the sun's
rays creep over the edge of the horizon and light up the sky, feeling
closer to my sister every time I watched it. I also went on a trip to
the Great Barrier Reef in the weeks after she died, a trip I had
planned before we lost her. I nearly didn't go on it but Mum encouraged me to go and do something for me again. I'm so glad I went.
The beauty of the vast, crystal blue water sprinkled with bright
vibrant coral left me in awe.

Breathing fresh air can help increase the oxygen levels in your
brain, which in turn increases serotonin, and the vitamin D we
receive from the sun is also a mood booster. Couple it with even a
short stroll outside, and you're also going to boost your endorphin
levels, which helps reduce any toxic emotions weighing you down.
When you're in a better headspace, it's easier to manage your
thoughts and regulate your feelings.

If we stop, put our phones down and look around, we'll see how
nature in all of its vast beauty does a wonderful job of putting things

into perspective, and that even though what we're going through in our personal world may be tough, it's still just an experience in *our* world and there's this vast and amazing *entire* world that's out there ready and waiting for us to explore it. Whether it's as simple as driving to a lake to put your feet in the water or as elaborate as a spontaneous last-minute trip to the Mediterranean, my message is that when you're feeling caught up with what's happening in your world, get outside and let the natural world inspire yet humble you. Let nature use its natural healing benefits, as well as its effortless ability to make you go "wow," to help you step back and see the *bigger* picture of how blessed we are to be alive. In big and small ways, nature gives us miracles and moments to remind us of that. It's up to us to soak them up and appreciate them to help us get the rush of healthy serotonin chemicals we need to get through the tough days.

*   *   *

So there you have it! That's your list of go-to activities you can do when you're feeling really low and want to give your headspace a boost. If you haven't tried some of these suggestions yet, I encourage you to be open-minded in giving them a go. See how you feel after trying them out. Or maybe you used to do a lot of these suggestions as part of your daily routine, like going to the gym daily or journaling often, but now you're feeling so low or rocked by life, you're not ready to return to your everyday routine yet. Maybe you can't imagine finding the motivation to go to a CrossFit class or volunteer at your local animal shelter. That makes it tempting to go to the other extreme of curling up on the couch and hiding away in another season of *Grey's Anatomy*. This may temporarily satisfy your brain with some dopamine from consuming some good entertainment, but behavior that requires very little effort or social connection ends up making our life feel emptier and unfulfilled.

Doing what's easy all the time ends up making our life harder because it strips us of purpose and growth. So while I'm not against a night every so often of binge watching *Grey's* or scrolling on social media, we want to balance out getting our dopamine from doing something that might not be pleasurable in the moment but feels good once it's done. That's the kind of behavior that really benefits your headspace in a lasting way.

So to get momentum going with these healthier habits, we need to drop the "all or nothing" mentality—the idea that we have to do everything perfectly and to the extreme—that often stops us from doing anything at all because it feels like too much. There is an alternative that I call the "all or *something*" mentality—the reality that doing something is always better than nothing. Doing a ten minute walk around the block before work is better than snoozing the alarm two extra times and not giving yourself a healthy dose of endorphins and dopamine. Having a coffee with a friend is better than staying holed up inside and missing out on the good feelings of oxytocin and serotonin. The key to taking care of yourself, especially when you're going through hard times, is to commit to doing at least *something* every day that you might not feel like doing in the moment, but on the other side of doing it, you feel better for having done it due to the happy chemicals it releases for your mind and body.

So now I want you to think about what are those things that you tend to feel better after doing (even if they suck in the moment)? It doesn't matter if they feel a little too much for you to do right now, but grab a notebook or open up your Notes app, and on a new page, write out three to five things that you know are typically a mood booster for you based on what's been suggested throughout this chapter already. Is it watching the sunrise? Baking banana bread? Going for a jog? Coffee out with a friend?

Once you've written those three to five things, look at your list: which feel doable right now as they are? It's okay if none of them do. When we're really struggling, it's natural to feel overwhelmed by our usual routine and want to retreat away. But then remember, that robs us of the feel-good chemicals that these activities usually give us, right at a time when we could really use them! So rather than letting yourself go all the way to the "I just won't do anything" option, let's create "something" goals for each of the activities you listed. To change your "all" goal into a "something" goal, break it down into bite-size pieces until it feels doable for where you're at right now. For example, if going for a 5k jog usually lifts your spirits, but your heart and body feel heavy with stress or heartbreak, reduce it down to what does feel doable: perhaps walking 5ks or even just walking for ten minutes around the block. Sure, it might not release the same amount of endorphins and dopamine as the 5k jog, but it's still going to release more than just sitting curled up in a ball on the couch. Something is better than nothing 100 percent of the time.

Another example might be going out for a coffee with a friend— you're physically feeling run down from long days at work, and your eyes are puffy from crying, so the thought of being out in public sounds daunting. But rather than just ghosting her message and crawling into bed to binge-watch YouTube, the "something" option may be to ask if she can come over for a chat and grab two coffees on the way. I did that so often in the weeks after Nicole died—friends would kindly offer to take me out for lunch or coffee, which most days felt too daunting to be out in the overstimulating world of a cafe, but I knew the company of a friend or someone to talk to would do me good. So I'd often ask them to come to my place instead. I'd still cry and struggle my way through some of the conversations, or we'd talk about completely mundane things like who was playing football that night or what my friend was doing that weekend, but I always felt better on the other side of our small chats. I know that taking the "something" option over the "nothing" option of things that were good for my well-being helped my brain release just enough of the healthy chemicals that managing my thoughts and processing my emotions was possible.

So look back over your list of things that typically help you feel better after you do them, and look at how you can reduce them to doable activities that you think you can manage this week. These are your "something" goals that you can focus on when you're feeling lost in the fog of your own negative headspace and need something to help you balance it out in a healthier way. You might not feel like doing them in the moment, but I hope by explaining the brain chemistry throughout this chapter about why they're worth doing for how you'll feel *after* doing them, helps you tap into your own determination to do these things anyway and reap the rewards!

In the final chapter of this book, I'll recap everything you've learned and teach you how to use the 3 Rs in a whole new way, because not only can the hard things about our past hold us back, but our worries about the hard things that may happen in our future. So let's look at how we can use the 3 Rs to create resilience ahead of time to help you live your best life!

LOOKING AHEAD

Making the Changes You
Want with the 3 Rs

In this final chapter, I'd like to take the 3 Rs I've been teaching you and apply them in a different way. Traditionally, when we think of resilience, we think about how we respond to events or situations that have already happened in our lives. But the 3 Rs strategy is also one you can use to navigate and prepare for challenges or big changes *before* they occur. Because sometimes life is hard not because of something that's happened, but because of something that hasn't.

Have you ever stayed in a job, relationship, or situation you didn't really *want* to be in, but you were scared to leave it because of the fear of "what if?" Maybe you wanted to make a change, but thought *"What if everyone judges me for it?"* or *"What if I don't find another job?"* or *"What if this is as good as it gets?"*

In my early twenties, that fear of "what if?" kept me in a relationship for a year longer than I really wanted to be in it. My heart had moved on, but I was worried that if I left, I'd be making a huge mistake, and was concerned that he and all my family would hate me for breaking his heart. This fearful mind chatter kept me clinging to that relationship. I get how easy it is to spiral into all the "what if's?" and end up retreating from making any changes that your heart desires but your mind fears.

In fact, it happens more often than we might think. Bogged down with the weight of expectations from parents, bosses, friends, and the elusive online world, research shows as many as 70 percent of young adults have experienced a quarter-life crisis and a sense of purposelessness. In your twenties and thirties, you're starting to tick off boxes that society says will make you successful, like graduating from college, finding a significant other, and landing a stable job with good financial security. Yet maybe, like I did, you're not experiencing the fulfillment or satisfaction that you were sold would come with it. There's a smile on your face, but a tension or restlessness in your heart. Maybe you've got the nice car you once dreamed of being able to afford, or a partner whose stellar looks belong on the cover of a magazine, but something still feels missing. You dread going to work, even though it was once your dream job. You're bored during conversations over dinner with your partner, even though they're dreamy to look at. Or maybe you haven't even got close to achieving any of the things your fresh-out-of-college-self thought was possible for you, and you're feeling in a slump.

Usually this is because somewhere along the line we've made choices from a place of pressure or chasing status or money, and not in alignment with our core values, talents, and interests. Dylan, one of my coaching clients, was a quality control manager for a living, yet when we did some deeper diving, he revealed his love for woodworking and sculpting. He was an artist by heart and a structured manager by day. It made sense to me why he was starting to feel a little empty in his daily life if there was nowhere for that creativity in his job.

Then there was Lyla, who was in a long-term relationship with a guy her family loved. She was feeling so much angst because she knew he was going to propose soon but she personally struggled to connect with him on things other than their shared love of fitness and good wine. "He's nice, but . . ." kept coming up in our coaching sessions together, as if she had to keep talking herself into staying and into leaving all at the same time. She felt confused, scared, and hopeless. Even though she had so many choices and her whole future ahead of her, it felt like her fear had already planned out the rest of her life to be in a relationship she didn't want.

It's much easier said than done to take a leap that feels scary to you. No matter how much you might pep talk yourself before you hit "send" on your resignation email or before you walk into your living room to tell your partner it's over, your fears come rumbling back at you louder than ever, and before you know it, you're deleting the email or asking your partner what they'd like for dinner. The fear of the unknown, the fear of being judged harshly, the fear of failing at a new pursuit: fear is the biggest barrier I've found that keeps us stuck in an unfulfilled place.

Fear is the biggest barrier I've found that keeps us stuck in an unfulfilled place.

Given I've just spent a whole book explaining how much our mindset creates our experience of a circumstance, I think it's important to mention here that yes, you can technically create your own happiness and fulfillment in any circumstance you're given. The difference is, are you making that decision to stay in your current circumstances from a place of faith and acceptance? Or a place of fear and avoidance?

Many times life will throw us into a situation we can't control or change, like the death of a loved one, a scary prognosis, or a break up. That's where stepping up to find purpose and meaning within the "suck" of the circumstance is helpful. It's helping you practice the faith and courage that even though you can't control your external world, internally you can still control your response to it. You're not avoiding reality; you're accepting it. That's what this book has been about so far. But typically what's beneath our sense of feeling lost or unfulfilled are not tragic, life altering circumstances you didn't see coming—they're big and small decisions you've made over time from a place of fear or lack of clarity that's taken you way off course from your true calling in life.

I'm so excited to help you put the 3 Rs into practice to conquer your fears and be resilient in the face of challenges and changes that you're making *on your own terms.*

Recognize Where Fear Is Keeping You Stuck

When I was twenty, I was spinning over the decision over whether to leave my corporate job to take on my sister's charity full time and pursue my dream as a speaker. I was afraid of letting my parents down, that no schools would want to book me, and looking like a fool to everyone who already thought I was crazy for leaving my job in the first place. I felt a lot of fear ahead of making that life change, and I've felt it many times since. Uprooting my entire career to move to the United States and pay thousands in lawyer fees to go for a work visa that I had no guarantee of getting was also terrifying.

So starting with the first "R" in our three-step resilience strategy, Recognize your thoughts, it's time to peel back the layers and get clear *where* fear is holding you back from making a change you desire, and *what* that specific fear is.

The three main fears I see that keep people spiraling into avoidance and inaction are:

- Fear of being judged and what other people think: *"I'm just worried everyone will think I'm flakey if I change jobs again."*
- Fear of rejection and failing: *"No one will even listen to my podcast if I launch it. What's the point in trying?"*

- Fear of the unknown and uncertainty: *"What if we break up and then I don't find anyone else better?"*

Which of these three fears—fear of being judged, of rejection, or of uncertainty—do you notice are keeping you stuck in a situation you don't want to be in right now? Maybe it's some of all three of these fears. There's only one way to find out. Grab a journal or open up the Notes section of your phone and answer these questions:

1. Where in life am I feeling restless or unfulfilled? Why do you think that is?
2. If I had all the courage in the world and wasn't worried about failing or other people's opinions, what's a life change I'd make or a goal I'd go after that I'm currently procrastinating on?
3. Why am I not making that change now? What am I really afraid of happening?

I don't want you just answering these questions in your mind as you read along, I really want you to take the time to reflect on these questions and write down your honest answers to them to really reveal to yourself exactly what's going on in your internal world and where your fear is blocking you from taking action on what matters to you.

When I ask these types of questions in my coaching sessions, there are two main answers I initially get back from my clients. The first being something like, "Oh I don't know what I really want. I don't know if now is the right time. I don't know how to even go about it."

Now on the surface, "I don't know" sounds like a legitimate excuse to not be taking action. And it may actually be true—you may not be sure what change you want to make in your life or how to make it happen. And if that's you, that's OK. There's just one shift I want you to make in that thinking: "I'm not sure, *yet*." Don't put a period at the end of "I don't know" as if it's a dead end. Instead, add "yet" to the end of that thought and then tell yourself, "Just take a guess." As we explored in Chapter 9, reminding yourself to just take a guess often helps you tap into so much more of your own wisdom and truth because a guess is just about putting something out there without needing it to be "right" so we stop shutting ourselves down in fear of being wrong or being judged. Because I've found more often than not "I don't know" is typically fear in disguise. It's easier to pretend to be confused or unsure, than it is to admit "I'm really freaking terrified of leaving my job or moving away from my family."

It's important to recognize it's not confusion but the fear beneath that is keeping you paralyzed from taking action, because solving for fear is very different than solving for confusion.

I want to make clear, I'm not judging you for feeling afraid of daring to go after something that's way beyond your comfort zone. We feel these fears not because we're not ready to make a change in our lives or because we're weak or unprepared; it's because we have a human brain wired for survival. Change is unfamiliar to the brain—it can't predict what potential dangers or threats may come up as well as it can on the familiar path you're currently on. So naturally, your brain will seize up in fear when we make a change and try to cling back on to the "certain" path that it knows.

Your survival brain has also been conditioned to fear being rejected or judged by others because we are a tribal species. We depended on working together as a tribe to survive. If we were rejected by one of our fellow tribesmen or judged as not worthy of being in the group, we'd be left alone to fend for ourselves, which would've meant certain death back in caveman days. So fear of rejection, failure, and judgment is as much a part of your humanness as your

Fear coming up before a big change is natural, but whether it holds you back is a choice.

heartbeat is. Do not let that derail you. If you wait for your fears to pass before making a change, be ready for your life to pass you by and for it to be too late. Fear coming up before a big change is natural, but whether it holds you back is a choice.

Reflect on How You're Uncomfortable Avoiding the Change

Now that you've recognized the fear beneath your indecision and inaction, it's time to do the next R of Reflecting upon the impact this fear is having on your life. Identifying your fears doesn't magically dissolve them. In fact, the opposite usually happens: our brain, being the survival machine that it is, starts to justify those fears even more and tries to convince you to stay right where you are. We need to silence those ANTs by showing your brain what your desperate attempts to avoid risk and discomfort are costing you.

Going back to my coaching client, Lyla, who was feeling suffocated in her current relationship and really wanted to move on from the guy she knew wasn't the one. She'd spent yet another half of our session telling me how unhappy she felt. So one day, I told her, this week is the week: you need to be honest and end things with him. Instantly, she clamped up and said "Ohh, but I just don't think I can. It's just so hard to hurt his feelings."

I told her that it's also hard not to tell him the truth. I knew she was afraid of the discomfort of being vulnerable and saying something that might break his heart. But there was no way around discomfort in this situation: either she was going to do it through taking action from her values and ending things with him, or she was going to feel the discomfort of letting her fears dictate her life

and then be stuck feeling resentful, unfulfilled, and in a relationship she doesn't even want to be in. There's heartbreak either
way—it's either his heart or her heart. And there's nothing worse
than breaking your own by saying "no" to the things you really
want in life.

I got a text a few days later from her telling me that she did it,
and that it was hard, but she did it. And she felt so relieved that
she did. That's the power of reflecting on your fears and seeing how
despite their pleas to stay in your "comfort zone," making choices
out of fear actually leads to more discomfort in life. Because of all
the voices in the world, the one voice you can't silence is the one
in your own mind. It will keep eating away at you and often com-
pels self-defeating action like overdrinking, overeating, scrolling
online endlessly, or living out our lives through the characters on
the show we're binge watching on Netflix. As we learned earlier in
the book, that may temporarily drown out the desire for something
more, but long term, it leads to more issues and struggles with your
health, relationships, work performance, and overall happiness in
life. There is nothing more uncomfortable than not following your
own heart or curiosity.

So now it's your turn to reflect on your specific situation and
the fear that's keeping you stuck from taking action on it. Take a
few moments to journal in response to this question: What result
is your fear *really* creating for you? It might seem like you'd be comfortable staying where you are or to keep doing what you're doing.
However, are you really happy? Do you feel fulfilled? Or do you feel
an internal struggle or angst?

For example, if you're dissatisfied with your job, staying there
might help you avoid the temporary stress that you may go through
if you had to start job hunting or face rejection from another
employer. But by staying at your current job, you're having to con-
tinuously face stresses that might be lowering your quality of life.

Maybe your boss makes you work overtime and micromanages every project so you never have the space to grow at what you're doing. Or maybe you have to keep dealing with being stuck in traffic during your one hour commute to work that's slowly grinding away your sanity at the end of each work day.

Or maybe you're itching to move to a new city. If you stay where you are, you may avoid the temporary sadness you could feel if you moved away from your family and had to start building a whole new network of friends in a new town. But by staying where you currently live, you're dealing with the restlessness of seeing the same downtown every day with the same people who talk about the same things every weekend that you go out.

Or maybe you are ready to start dating again after a tough break-up. If you don't give dating a try, you may avoid the temporary feeling of anxiety that comes with starting online dating and meeting new people. But by not putting yourself out there, you're missing out on finding that person who makes everything in life—whether it's a trip to the grocery store or a vacation to Paris—feel even better simply because you're doing it with them. Although you may be living a full and amazing life being single, if you're avoiding getting into another relationship out of fear of being hurt again, you're just hurting yourself ahead of time by not even giving yourself a chance.

Comfort zones aren't really that comfortable when you reflect on how they really feel. Meanwhile, the discomfort we feel when we're bravely going after a new goal or making a big change gives us something back in the sense that we're actually taking action. And every time we take action, there's some value to be gained because humans learn most through experience.

By reflecting on the impact of hiding from your fears, you reveal to your brain there is no "comfortable" path in life; either you're uncomfortable putting in the effort to create an outcome you want, or you avoid the discomfort upfront through temporary distractions and end up stuck with an uncomfortable outcome you don't want. So if you're going to be uncomfortable either way, wouldn't you rather choose discomfort that keeps you moving forward rather than discomfort that only keeps you stuck?

Redirect to Three Empowering Truths That Inspire Courage to Make a Change

So far we've recognized the fear keeping you stuck and reflected on how letting your fear dictate your choices brings short-term relief and long-term discomfort. So it's not about trying to find a comfortable path in life, because there are none. It's about choosing the discomfort that brings you closer to your goals, your values and the kind of person you want to be.

Now it's time to use the third and final R, to Redirect your brain to a place where you find the strength to do exactly that: to take action on your goals and desired change, even though you may still feel really scared to do so. Remember, it's not about being fearless, as that's trying to be superhuman and is only possible in movies. In real life, your humanness means fear will come up ahead of any uncertain change or risk you take. So stop waiting for your fears to fade away; instead, find the courage to take them with you by redirecting to these three empowering truths that are helpful to hold on to when it comes to living a life that's worth the struggle.

Truth #1: People most regret the things they don't do

Whether it's asking your cute gym instructor out for coffee or taking that position at a new company overseas, it's easy to let anxiety about all the bad things that could happen take over for so long that we end up missing the chance to do that thing at all. By letting the opportunity pass you by, have you just avoided your biggest regret, or walked head first into it?

According to research by author Daniel Pink, who collected over 23,000 regrets from people around the world, people's biggest regrets tend to be the things they *don't* do. Even more so than the things that didn't work out as they'd hoped. I believe there are two main reasons for this:

REASON 1: YOUR BRAIN CAN'T CLOSE THE LOOP ON "WHAT IF?"

Remember, your brain loves to close an open loop in its circuitry and return back to a state of closure and certainty. The problem is, your brain will never be able to close the loop on "What if I . . . asked that guy out?" or ". . . took that job?" or ". . . left this relationship five years ago?" It can never close the loops on those what if's if that stuff never happened! You will never know whether that barista was your perfect life partner or if that job in a new city would have led you to a more fulfilling career path. And your brain hates the tension of not knowing. It will spin over and over it for as long as you live trying to close a loop that it can't close with certainty. So give yourself closure by taking action on what matters to you. Do it scared. Do it unsure. Do it while you still can.

Do it scared. Do it unsure. Do it while you still can.

I personally experienced this when I decided to still take on the corporate position I had landed right out of university. I landed the job while my sister was still alive, and I was meant to move to a new state for it in January—just eight weeks after she'd passed away. That felt way too soon for me, and I began to question, "Should I even take on this job at all? Am I ready for it so soon after losing Nicole?" And then I did what I always recommend to my clients before a big life change: ask for advice from people you respect who have some experience with what you're struggling with and hear out their perspective on it. After talking with my Dad and brother about it, I decided that I didn't want to quit this opportunity before I gave it a chance and actually discovered for myself (rather than just overthinking it in my brain) whether that career path was the right fit for me.

The company kindly rearranged my position so I could stay in my home city, and I began the job at the end of January. Although I didn't feel a strong connection to the job, and I ended up resigning just ten weeks later, I am so glad I did decide to take on the opportunity, because now I know that wasn't the job for me. I actually experienced it for myself and can now close the "What if I'd actually tried out that career path?" loop in my brain. Which has been very helpful with my resilience in my speaking and coaching career, because running your own business is not for the faint-hearted—it can be a lot of pressure with long hours and all the responsibility rests with you—but knowing what it felt like for me to work in a corporate environment, I'm not "what if-ing" my other life had I'd taken on the job. I know I'm on the path that's most meaningful to me. That's what's given me so much determination to persevere through challenging months in my career, especially early on, when I was barely scraping by, or when I was spending hours emailing potential gigs only to hear nothing back. That was hard, but I didn't quit or go back to the corporate world. Because I know the alternative wouldn't have been any more fulfilling for me. So I'm able to stop my brain spiraling into a made-up fantasy of how much better that job could've been or drown in regret. I know I wasn't happy in that job, so I can move on from it.

REASON 2: TAKING ACTION ALWAYS BRINGS VALUE
The truth is, there's no guarantee how anything will work out. You may end up really missing the ex you broke up with. Your new small

business may tank after a year. You might have to hear "I told you so" from your judgmental parents who thought you were crazy for starting your own business in the first place. You may fail. Be hurt. Get rejected. Suffer humiliation. All of that can and may happen. However, that still is a better case scenario than the alternative of having not taken a chance on those things at all. Because there's nothing to be gained from doing nothing and living life in avoidance of what your heart feels called to do.

Taking action on those things, on the other hand, will always bring some sort of value because of what you learn and experience along the way. Even when it turns out to be a complete mess, at least you know you avoided your biggest regret of never knowing. You can weave any experience in your life, even the most painful or humiliating ones, into a meaningful, growth-worthy experience. But you cannot turn back time. No one on Earth is that powerful. So you'll forever be stuck with the regret of never knowing, while if you take action, you still may not get the outcome you want, but you will always gain in some way.

Stepping up, taking action, putting yourself out there to go after a goal or make a change is always going to require courage. So immediately you're already gaining something from that situation. Because every time you practice courage in life, you grow your capacity to feel uncomfortable and do something meaningful with your life. There's no greater skill to practice than knowing how to do brave things in alignment with your values. That's what builds character and creates fulfillment. Always doing what's easy may be good for our ego, but it's struggle and doing hard things that are good for our growth.

In fact, that's what Daniel Pink's research also found—what people regret the most isn't just that they miss that opportunity, but they miss the potential growth that comes with those opportunities and experiences. They miss and grieve the person that they could have become had they taken on that experience because of the way experiences lead to lessons and growth.

So when your brain fears everything you could lose before handing in your resignation to dive into taking your side hustle on full time or spiral into the fear you'll never find anyone who makes you happier if you end this relationship, be sure to redirect it to what you could gain. I can't say for sure what that gain will be, but it will always be something.

For example, doing things before you feel 100 percent ready (because often, you never will!), can teach you where there's a huge gap in where your skillset is now and where it needs to be. Maybe you take a chance on your dream to be a motivational speaker and book yourself a gig that turns out to fall pretty flat with the audience. *"Okay, so it turns out I'm not as great at public speaking yet as I thought I was. But now I know I need to put my head down and keep practicing my public speaking skills and should join something like Toastmasters."* Sure, that moment of standing up in front of an audience and mind-blanking on your speech and feeling like a deer in the headlights is not fun, but it's not without purpose. You've now learned there's more to work on and develop to achieve your dream, but you wouldn't know that if you never attempted it. Overthinking things will not bring clarity, only valued action does. That's what brings the wisdom and awareness we can't gain when we're letting fear stop us.

Another gem that I've realized you can gain by living true to your values rather than your fears is the friendships you can make along the way. I was nervous to join Pilates in my new hometown because I hadn't done a Pilates class in over ten years and didn't know anyone in the class. I had all the fearful thoughts: *"What if they judge me? What if they think I'm weird or really bad at it?"* I couldn't talk myself out of the nerves (remember: they'll naturally show up whenever we try new things), so I decided I'd just do it scared. And boy, I'm glad I did. I really enjoy Pilates but more than anything I'm loving the new friends I've made that have helped fill a void I'd be feeling of a lack of girlfriends in my life. Working on my own business at home every day hadn't given me much of a chance to meet new people. So while I thought I was joining Pilates to gain flexibility and strength, I've actually gained more in friendships and my sense of belonging.

I want you to stay open to those possibilities in your life, too. For another example, maybe you might think you're being called to apply to graduate school because of a career ambition, but maybe there's more to it than meets the eye in terms of friendships and bringing new meaningful experiences into your life.

And if I'm having a hard time convincing you that there actually is something to be gained from every chance you take on making a change in your life, then maybe at the very least what you learn is what I learned with my first corporate job—that it definitely isn't the right path or person for you. Discovering what isn't for you is just as valuable as discovering what is.

My sister showed me this when she left the New Zealand Ballet at sixteen years old. To dance there was a dream she'd begged Mum and Dad for relentlessly and she couldn't have been more excited when they finally let her go at the end of tenth grade. A few months in, we could see she wasn't loving it because it was much more structured and regimented than her free spirit needed. Within six months, she decided to come back home to Australia, and I'd never been prouder of my sister than that moment. She really taught me the power of taking a chance on something you'd worked hard for and then also not being too proud to change your mind when it wasn't what you thought it would be. She told me she had no regrets because she knew that wasn't what she wanted to keep striving for and needed to find something with more freedom and creativity to it. She learned through taking a chance on her dreams, not through overthinking them on the sidelines.

Truth #2: People's opinions are a reflection of themselves and not something to take personally

"Oh don't worry, no one is judging you" is a sweet little thing you might hear a mother say to reassure someone stressing over what others think of them. That thought is nice in theory, but not accurate in everyday life. The reality is people do judge others; it happens automatically and is a part of how we make sense of the world and our place in it. You might be thinking about your opinionated uncle or nosy neighbor always giving their two cents on whether you're having kids yet or when you are going to quit that job. And the truth is, whether we mean to or not, we judge others, too. It's part of our human nature to judge, and it's going to happen just like the sun is going to rise tomorrow. We don't get a choice about that part, but we do get a choice about whether we let the fear of them judging us stop us from taking action on what matters to us.

The biggest reason we get so hung up on people judging us is because we take it so personally. And it seems like we have no other choice, because they are talking about us so it has to be *about* us, right? Wrong.

Let me give you a simple example as to why. Imagine you walk into a conference room of twenty people to do some networking. You're all in a big group chatting away, and they all see you act the same way, say the same thing, same body language, same outfit— they experience all of you for that thirty minutes. Now let's say you walk out of the room to grab some food, and I walk up to each person individually and say, "Hey, what did you think of the person who just walked out?" Now if you are the one *controlling* the opinion of what they think about you, they'll all have the *exact* same opinion of you. But they won't. You'll get twenty different opinions. You *know* this is true.

This is exactly what happens every time I stand up and speak in front of audiences, and if their opinions really were a direct reflection of what my talk was like and whether I'm a good speaker or not, then they'd all have the exact same opinion of my talk. But I can tell you they certainly don't. I've have students who are moved to tears or excitedly race up for a big thank you hug or send messages raving about how much they loved it, while other students look like they're about to die of boredom and would rather be anywhere else in the world.

How can this be? How can we each show up and act the same way, and be the same person and say the same things to a group of people, yet they each have a different opinion of us?

Because other people's opinions are about *them* (not you!). You might be wearing a jersey of a team they support so they immediately think you're awesome. You might have the same name as their ex and immediately are turned off by you. They might be feeling super insecure about how they look today so they're really judgmental about how you're looking. They might hate having to sit still for so long in a stuffy room and be hungry for lunchtime so they do not want to even listen to a speaker. Notice who all of this tells us about? Them.

Other people's opinions are about them, based on factors *beyond* your control: their upbringing, values, beliefs, past experiences, and, more often than not, their insecurities. Be ready for people to be particularly judgmental about your choices if you're daring to go after something they've wanted in their lives too, but they have been too afraid to do it.

So when you recognize and reflect on the fact that your main fear holding you back from going after something is what your best friend or family might think of it, redirect to this truth: No matter what you do or don't do with your life, people will have opinions about it. You might stay in a job you've wanted to leave to avoid upsetting your boss, and then your sister-in-law judges you for playing it too safe. You might start a podcast to document your experience with celiac disease after someone from your support group encouraged you to, and then your partner thinks you're exposing too much and just seeking attention. People will judge you regardless of what you do or don't do, and the challenge is not to take any of it personally. It's a reflection of who *they* are. Our choices and actions aren't going to be everyone's preference—and that's okay!

Now, I am not saying ignore every piece of advice you're given, as if people's opinions about what we're doing are never valid. I'm all for constructive feedback and seeking guidance from people you respect and have your best interests at heart when you're in need of support. But my rule in life is don't take criticism personally from someone you wouldn't seek advice from. More often than not, people are projecting their shortcomings and fears onto you. Especially parents and family members whose instincts are to protect us from harm, and some can't tolerate the idea of us struggling or failing at something. As if it would be unbearable if we failed, not realizing that failing at something we care about can be one of the most transformative experiences of our lives.

That's exactly what I had to remind myself of when making the biggest change in my life. Someone near and dear to me called me up the day I decided to quit my corporate job in an attempt to talk me out of doing it. He told me he thought I was crazy and making a huge mistake walking away from such a solid career path and good money, to go and work for a charity for free. From his perspective, that may have been true. But the thing is, that's just his perspective. And his perspective is based on the limits of *his* comfort zone and what *he* wants out of life. Not me. I wasn't about to let thoughts—which are literally sentences in someone else's brain—be the reason I don't pursue my passion in life. I'd rather be broke through my twenties than look back in my thirties and think, "I could've done something really special and meaningful in honor of my sister, but I was scared." That was what would be intolerable for me.

His words did sting temporarily. Because of course it's nice when the people in our lives believe in us and support our goals, but the reality is, not all people will. And that's okay. The only person who needs to believe in your dreams to make them happen, is you. Only you know how hard you're willing to work and how many times you're willing to fail to become successful, so let people judge you.

The only person who needs to believe in your dreams to make them happen, is you.

Let your mother think you're wrong for leaving your marriage. Let your boss think that your new business is doomed to fail. Let your best friend think that your move overseas is not worth the risk. And then remember that's a reflection of their comfort zone—which you're under no obligation to live within. Your obligation is to give yourself the most meaningful life possible during the short time you're here on Earth.

So when fear of judgment rears its ugly head and attempts to hold you back from taking action on that next goal, redirect to the fact that there's no hiding from judgment in life, so you might as well do what you want so you can win over the opinion that matters most—your own. True success is living life true to your own definition of success.

Truth #3: Don't flatline your life while you're still alive

I've realized that our lives are much like a heart monitor that you see in hospitals. Let me explain to you why. If you were to put your life on a scale of one to ten, where one is when you're experiencing really intense negative emotion like pain, stress, or humiliation and ten is where you're overjoyed with lots of positive emotion and fulfilled with deep sense of purpose and passion flowing in your veins, where would you rank your life? Do you often experience extreme highs and lows? Or somewhere in the middle—about a five to seven? Your life isn't terrible, but it isn't particularly fulfilling either. It's just good enough. Most people, I've found, live life in the latter— aiming for the—five to seven range of trying to create a life that doesn't risk much exposure to emotional extremes. If someone is healthy and alive, the monitor has very contrasting highs and lows. Yet when the monitor flatlines, it's a sign they're no longer living. How many of us are flatlining in our lives? How many of us are killing our dreams to try to play it safe and keep our emotions in the flatline range between—five and seven?

And it makes sense that we do that, because society ingrains into us that failure and struggling is a "bad thing," and we should aim to be "happy" all the time. But also, our brains are wired to avoid discomfort, including emotional discomfort. And as we've explored so far in the book, unless we start to practice using the 3 Rs to manage our automatic brain, many people just run off this default function, trying to make our lives as comfortable as they can be and avoiding making changes that could risk extreme negative emotion.

Now you may be thinking, "Ah, Kate—what's wrong with seeking the middle range of emotions and not want to risk extreme negative ones?" There's absolutely nothing wrong with it. But recognize what it costs you. Because in order to experience the deep overflowing sensation of fulfillment—those moments where your heart feels like it's about to burst with joy and love—you've got to also be all in on those moments where your heart feels on fire. Like it's been stabbed. Like it's been torn out of your chest with grief.

You've got to be all in on feeling what it feels like to fail, to be told no, to be laughed at and ridiculed, to be judged a mistake or a failure, to be rejected. To be told you're not good enough. To be told nothing at all because no one is even paying attention no matter how hard you try. You've got to be all in on feeling the worst of humanity at a zero or one in order to experience the best of it at a nine or a ten.

Those feelings of pure fulfillment and satisfaction don't come from avoiding the ones or zeros, but from overcoming them. From enduring them. From rising above them. Your life reaches new heights in joy because of the depths of your lows. Sometimes that pain comes from things beyond our control, like losing my sister; there wasn't a thing I could do about that, and I was thrown into the deep end of that grief. I know you're reading this book because life in one way or another has done the same to you, too. But that experience taught me that we live in a world of contrast, so as my heart is wrenched into new depths of pain, I have the capacity to experience new heights of joy, even in the simplest of things: a good belly laugh, watching the snow fall, my dog's goofy tail wag. That lesson came from a pain I couldn't control, but it taught me to move toward pain I can control because of what you gain from it. Purposely risk hitting the pits of zero or one on the scale of your emotions, because that's what takes your joy and fulfillment to the emotional heights of nine or ten.

This is why after losing my sister and the harsh wake-up call of how short life is, I chose to create a life that involves moments of zero to one on the emotional scale so I can reach new peaks of nines and tens. I could have chosen to stay in that "safe" job that guaranteed me a five to six because I wasn't dealing with the risk of failing as a speaker for my sister's charity, but I would've missed out on feeling the fulfillment that comes when I step off stage and realize I did the very thing that terrified me and hopefully helped

a life while I was at it. I could have chosen to stay in that safe relationship with someone from my hometown that guaranteed me a
five to six, where I was never dealing with loneliness and aching
feeling of being on the other side of the world from my now husband, but it also meant I would not have experienced the heights
of pure love and joy that come from being in his arms knowing what
we've overcome to make it happen. I could have said no to writing
this book so I don't have to risk any judgment about what I share
and my personal experiences, but then I would miss out on the sur-
real pride and joy I'll feel when I finally hold this book in my
hands. I have chosen to embrace a life that leads to extremes:
extreme grief and extreme joy. Extreme pain and extreme fulfillment. Extreme failures and extreme success. I have chosen a life of
extremes, and I'm not talking about jumping out of a plane or physical kind of extreme. I'm talking about a life of emotional extreme.
Because to not choose emotional extreme means to not choose my
dreams or my values. I would instead be flatlining my life.

Benjamin Franklin once said, "Many people die at 25 and aren't
buried until they're 75." And it's a sad reality for so many of us. We're
killing off the heartbeat of our own desires and dreams by not being
willing to risk the emotional extremes that may come with it. And
yes, by taking the "safe" path and not daring to make that change
or chase after that big goal, you might avoid the temporary extreme
emotion that comes with failure, judgment or rejection, but you're
missing out on the feeling of fulfillment, thrill, and purpose that
comes from overcoming those things.

And that's why one last powerful thing to redirect to when your
fears are loud and trying to talk you into avoidance and inaction is
the metaphor of a heart monitor. To commit to a life that is in
alignment with *your* values and desires, and embracing the highs
and lows that come with that path, because just like on a heart rate
monitor, that's the sign of being alive. That's a sign of you being

brave with your days. No one is entitled to a life filled with the highs of only nines and tens all the time. What we are entitled to is using our ability to recognize, reflect, and redirect our responses, to find our way through the pits of zeros and ones and earn our way to creating wondrous moments filled with the highs of nines and tens. The world will not just drop that fulfillment in our lap; that is something we create for ourselves by taking responsibility for our own lives and the choices we are making in it, every minute of every day.

Throughout this book, I've given my very best to help you take responsibility for your response-ability in a way that gives you back power over your life. Whether it's to heal from a past heartbreak, overcome the struggle of a current hardship, or prepare for future challenges that may come through your own brave choices or through the world hitting us with the unexpected, I hope you now understand why you are never completely helpless over how you respond. Circumstances, thoughts, and feelings will happen automatically and many are natural in the initial reaction to what you've been forced to deal with. But neither your pain from your past nor your fear about your future should dictate the choices you make in your life. You are built for more than that. Through using the strategy of recognizing, reflecting, and redirecting, you can gain control over your response to shape your life for the better.

Neither your pain from your past nor your fear about your future should dictate the choices you make in your life.

I want to remind you to be patient with yourself as you practice these 3 Rs and know that you're always going to be human, which means struggle is a natural part of your existence. But turning that struggle into strength is a matter of focusing your efforts on what you can control and change, which I hope this book has shown you is always, at the very least, your own perspective.

On November 2, 2012, a Lee Ann Womack song played out across the oval where we hosted my sister's memorial. It was the song I chose in dedication to her because all the lyrics captured the essence of Nicole and everything she taught me. They're the words I want to leave you with, too, because I know this world can sometimes feel so awful. But it's our world, the only one we've been given in this lifetime and I want you to use these 3 Rs to give you the resilience to live it to the fullest. Or, as the lyrics sang out while I took small shaky steps around the oval in honor of my sister that day, here is what I wish for you above all else:

"When you get the choice to sit it out or dance, I hope you dance."

RESOURCES

While you've finished reading *Okay, Now What?*, my support doesn't end here! To find out more information about my life-coaching services or if you are interested in having me speak at your event, please visit my website, www.kategladdin.com. Remember, you can also access free worksheets and  journal pages exclusive to this book using this QR code or going to okaynowhatbook.com.

In the following pages, I share some of my favorite resilience resources you can check out for extra support.

Feelings List

This list will help you identify your feelings for exercises and prompts throughout the book:

Confident	Anxious	Lonely
Happy	Hopeless	Incapable
Courageous	Devastated	Hateful
Curious	Overwhelmed	Upset
Calm	Lost	Annoyed

(Continued)

Feelings List (*Continued*)

Grateful	Angry	Distrustful
Loving	Hurt	Disappointed
Inspired	Infuriated	Guilty
Motivated	Heartbroken	Vulnerable
Determined	Ashamed	Pathetic
Optimistic	Powerless	Hateful
Excited	Weak	Resentful
Hopeful	Embarrassed	Empty
Amazed	Scared	Fatigued
Liberated	Worried	Panicked
Glad	Frustrated	Desperate
Understanding	Distressed	Grief
Accepting	Confused	Rejected
Compassionate	Weary	Lifeless
Forgiving	Impulsive	Doubtful
Kind	Skeptical	Alienated

Values List

Use this list to help you choose your top five core values:

Achievement	Faith	Experience
Ambition	Helpfulness	Respect
Competitiveness	Justice	Wisdom
Education	Kindness	Resilience
Hard Work	Passion	Bravery
Reliability	Friendship	Courage
Recognition	Belonging	Determination
Resourcefulness	Caring	Optimism
Balance	Family	Perseverance
Winning	Forgiveness	Self-Reliance
Adventure	Health	Growth
Creativity	Honesty	Charity

Curiosity	Love	Challenge
Freedom	Intelligence	Community
Fun	Thoughtfulness	Simplicity
Independence	Leadership	Dependability
Risk-Taking	Assertiveness	Fairness
Spontaneity	Decisiveness	Generosity
Contribution	Enthusiasm	Loyalty
Compassion	Strength	Open-Mindedness
Empathy	Integrity	Humor

Further Reading

For all my book lovers out there, here are some books I can recommend as a worthwhile read to keep building your resilience and mindset skills:

- For a truly eye-opening and awe-inspiring read, I highly recommend Holocaust survivor Eddie Jaku's powerful book, *The Happiest Man on Earth*.
- Another book just as impactful in realizing the strength of the human spirit to rise above the unthinkable, is *The Choice: Embrace the Possible* by Dr. Edith Eva Eger.
- Rachel Hollis's book, *Didn't See That Coming: Putting Life Back Together When Your World Falls Apart*, is a fun and insightful read filled with stories to inspire your perseverance and grit through life's unexpected setbacks.
- I love Mel Robbins's book, *The 5 Second Rule*, for more strategies and insights into managing your negative thought spirals and taking back control over your actions when you're feeling in a slump.
- For those who have also been blindsided by grief and want some further support and tips on healing after losing

someone you love, I highly recommend Sheryl Sandberg and Adam Grant's book *Option B: Facing Adversity, Building Resilience, and Finding Joy.*

- For another great book on taking better care of your mental health and managing your emotions, I recommend Dr. Julie Smith's book, *Why Has No One Told Me This Before?*

Further Listening

If you're like me and love listening to podcasts, here are some of my favorite self-help shows :

- *Okay. Now What?*—Hosted by yours truly! Tune in to learn more tools, strategies, and inspiration on all things resilience, self-help, motivation, relationships and confidence. I am also fortunate to have awesome guests who will inspire you with their stories and teach many nuggets of gold to help you live your best life!
- *Train Wreck Your Life*—Yes, this is the podcast show I was telling you about in Chapter 10! My amazing husband, Nate, and I chat openly about all things relationships and making tough life choices that people may deem crazy (like falling in love from opposite sides of the world! Filled with moments that don't make the highlight reel, we hope we'll have you snorting through your nose laughing in some shows while reaching for the tissues in others. Our goal is to help you deal with your mess ups in life with more humility, humor, and heart.
- *Modern Wisdom*: Hosted by English podcaster Chris Williamson, *Modern Wisdom* shares powerful lessons on life and psychology by the world's greatest thinkers to help you

better navigate the challenges of being human in an unpredictable world.

- *The Mel Robbins Podcast*: This podcast is a great listen for anyone who's interested in psychology and self-help, which given you're holding this book, I'm guessing is you! Mel has such a fun and relatable personality, and hosts a range of compelling guests who share the tools and inspiration to help you get more out of life.
- *The Life Coach School Podcast*: Hosted by the coach who certified me in life coaching, Brooke Castillo, this podcast dives even further into a lot of the mindset tools and resilience skills we explore in this book. Brooke's fun and feisty personality also makes it an entertaining listen!
- *Better Than Happy*: Hosted by fellow Life Coach School coach Jody Moore, this podcast covers relationships, health, emotions, mindset, confidence, entrepreneurship, and all the other hard parts about being human to help you live your most meaningful life.
- *Unf*ck Your Brain*: Hosted by Master Feminist Coach Kara Loewentheil, each episode teaches you how to shed the pressures of societal expectations, get clear on what *you* really want in life, and change your thinking to make sure you go get it.

Mental Health and Crisis Support

There are some deep and meaningful topics covered throughout this book. While I've done my best to provide insights and strategies I believe may be helpful, the content is not intended to be a substitute for professional advice, diagnosis, or treatment. Always seek the advice of your mental health professional or other qualified health provider with any questions you may have regarding your condition. If you're in crisis or having suicidal thoughts, please reach out for help:

National Suicide Prevention Lifeline 1-800-273-TALK (8255)

988 Mental Health Emergency Hotline: Calling 988 will connect you to a crisis counselor regardless of where you are in the United States.

NAMI's Teen & Young Adult HelpLine, for nationwide peer support and resource referrals. Text "Friend" to 62640; chat at nami .org/talktous; call 800-950-6264. Available Mondays through Fridays, 10 a.m. to 10 p.m. ET.

National Alliance for Eating Disorders Helpline: 1 (866) 662–1235. Monday–Friday, 9:00 AM–7:00 PM ET

ACKNOWLEDGMENTS

First and foremost, to my amazing editor, Laura—thank you for believing in my story and message so much that you offered me the opportunity to write this book. It's a dream come true to write a book like this in honor of my sister, and I couldn't think of a more awesome person to have by my side to get through it all. So many emails, Zoom calls, and hours of editing together—but we did it! You worked so hard to keep bringing out the best in my stories and strategies, and I appreciate you so much for seeing my bigger vision of the 3 Rs so clearly that it became the foundation of this book. I remember many years ago when I first created the 3 Rs as a strategy; I never thought I'd actually get to publish them! So again, thank you!

To my best friend and amazing husband, Nate. You make my life better in every way, especially on the long writing days when you're there for me to talk an idea through or help cook dinner because I'm working toward a deadline. Thank you for believing in me in the moments I struggle to believe in myself. I love the love that we share, and I hope it inspires other long-distance couples who read this book to keep believing in their relationship too—I'd go through all those days apart all over again just to have the incredible life we've built together in the mountains of Wyoming. It's heaven with you.

To my dog, Jaku, for being the best snuggle buddy on the cold writing days and being there to go for a walk with me when I got writer's block and needed a refresh. It helped lift my spirits up right when I needed it most, like only the love of a dog can.

Thank you to my coaching clients whom I've had the privilege of working with over the last six years—I never take for granted the opportunity to be your coach and that you trust me to help you through some of your toughest moments (and enjoy some good laughs together!). So much of the content and inspiration for this book comes from you guys and what I've learned through coaching with you all, so thank you for helping me grow as a coach and as a person.

To my wonderful friend Katie Shatusky—thank you for allowing me to share your inspiring story in my book and for the overall inspiration you bring to my life. I definitely believe that our friendship is one brought together by our angels and it's a true joy to know you and all of your Thumbs Up community.

To my Wyoming friends whom I was lucky enough to gain from starting Pilates—Candice, Allie, and Morgan—thanks for keeping my mind in a good place with our 6:00 AM classes and good giggles throughout my writing journey. It's my favorite way to start the day. And to my dear friend Stefanie—the incredible woman I have to thank for helping us buy our beautiful home in Wyoming, and who made us feel so welcomed as we settled in. Some parts of this book were quite emotional to write, but getting to write it beside the Big Horn mountains was so therapeutic.

To Deana—thank you for believing in me right from the very beginning of my career as a resilience speaker and life coach. When I reached out to you to design my website way back in 2017, you didn't miss a beat in putting together the most amazing site for me, and now with the new website for this book—you nailed it once again! Thanks for all the wisdom, guidance, and care you've given me over the years from one female business owner to another, I am very grateful to now call you my dear friend.

There are so many more people I want to thank for impacting my life in a positive way and supporting me throughout my writing this book and my career, but to finish with, I want to circle back around to the people I dedicated this book to—my Mum, Julie, and Dad, Vince. I hit the jackpot getting to be born into our Fitzy family and can't thank you enough for all your support—near or far. Dad, thank you for backing me 100 percent when I decided to leave my corporate job to pursue my dream to make a difference in the world through Nicole's legacy—and for having my back with it all ever since. And Mum, your dedication to helping make this dream come true—from 5:00 AM airport drop offs to get me to my next presentation and sending out countless emails to government contacts and high profile people through to helping me do some research for this book and cheering me on during weary days of writing and traveling—your dedication to being there for me, even now as an adult, has been the biggest blessing in my life. I know we all miss Nicole every single day, but seeing how you and Dad have picked up the pieces of our shattered family and found meaningful ways to live and enjoy life again in her honor, makes me so proud of you both—as I know Nicole would be also.

On the day we lost her, I posted a photo of us and wrote "A sister's bond is unbreakable." This book, written twelve years after her death, is proof of that. No matter how much time passes, my sister will always be my greatest inspiration and a part of every beat of my heart. Keep dancing on the clouds of heaven sis, until we meet again.

BIBLIOGRAPHY

Australian Government—Department of Foreign Affairs and Trade. "State of Play—Consular Services in 2022–23." March 2023. https://www.smartraveller.gov.au/.

Berezin, Gabriel, and Mika Liss. "The Neuroscience of Laughter, and How to Inspire More of It at Work." *NeuroLeadership Institute*. September 17, 2020. https://neuroleadership.com/your-brain-at-work/neuroscience-laughter-at-work/.

Bergeisen, Michael. "The Neuroscience of Happiness." *Greater Good*. September 22, 2010. https://greatergood.berkeley.edu/article/item/the_neuroscience_of_happiness.

Berman, Robby. "New Study Suggests We Have 6,200 Thoughts Every Day." *Big Think*. July 16, 2020. https://bigthink.com/neuropsych/how-many-thoughts-per-day/.

Boukobza, Philippe. "The Eye Sees Only What the Mind Is Prepared to Comprehend." *Visual Mapping*. September 15, 2012. https://www.visual-mapping.com/2012/09/the-eye-sees-only-what-mind-is-prepared.html.

"Buddha Quotes." *BrainyQuote.com*, BrainyMedia Inc. Accessed February 20, 2024. https://www.brainyquote.com/quotes/buddha_104025.

Clancy, Nicole. "Journaling Is Scientifically Linked to Happiness—Here Are 5 Easy Tips to Start Writing More." *Real Simple*. July 24, 2023. https://www.realsimple.com/health/mind-mood/journaling-increases-happiness#:~:text=Journaling%20thoughts%20and%20feelings%2C%20both.

Cleveland Clinic. "Dopamine." March 23, 2022. https://my.clevelandclinic.org/health/articles/22581-dopamine.

Dictionary.com. "What Doesn't Kill You, Makes You Stronger." *Everything after Z by Dictionary.com*, Everything After Z by Dictionary.com,

Mar. 2018, www.dictionary.com/e/slang/what-doesnt-kill-you-makes-you-stronger/.

Dorter, Greg. "Cognitive Fusion and Defusion in Acceptance and Commitment Therapy." *Greg Dorter Therapy* (blog). March 14, 2015. https://www.guelphtherapist.ca/blog/cognitive-fusion-defusion/#:~:text=Steven%20Hayes%2C%20who%20developed%20Acceptance.

Fallis, Jordan. "The 36 Best Ways to Naturally Increase Dopamine Levels in the Brain." *Optimal Living Dynamics.* October 17, 2023. https://www.optimallivingdynamics.com/blog/increase-dopamine-naturally.

Franklin, Benjamin. "Benjamin Franklin Quotes." *BrainyQuote.* N.d. https://www.brainyquote.com/quotes/benjamin_franklin_129949.

Gilmore, Joe. "The 10 Best Ways to Increase Dopamine Levels Naturally." *Gratitude Lodge.* October 31, 2023. https://www.gratitudelodge.com/the-10-best-ways-to-increase-dopamine-levels-naturally/.

Gotian, Ruth. "Your Biggest Regret May Be What You Did Not Do." *Forbes.* March 29, 2022. https://www.forbes.com/sites/ruthgotian/2022/03/29/your-biggest-regret-may-be-what-you-did-not-do/?sh=1c3cde71424b.

Haden, Jeff. "New Research Reveals What People Regret Most of All: 5 Ways to Make Sure You Never Do." *Inc.com.* June 4, 2018. https://www.inc.com/jeff-haden/new-research-reveals-what-people-regret-most-of-all-5-ways-to-make-sure-you-never-do.html.

Harvard Health Publishing. "Endorphins: The Brain's Natural Pain Reliever." *Harvard Health.* July 20, 2021. https://www.health.harvard.edu/mind-and-mood/endorphins-the-brains-natural-pain-reliever.

Henry Ford Health Staff. "Screen Time Limits Aren't Just for Kids. Why Adults Need Them Too." *Henry Ford Health.* December 14, 2021, www.henryford.com/blog/2021/12/adult-screen-time-limits.

Hill, Napoleon. "A Quote from Think and Grow Rich." *goodreads.com.* N.d. Accessed September 21, 2023. https://www.goodreads.com/quotes/659410-every-adversity-every-failure-every-heartbreak-carries-with-it-the.

McMah, Lauren. "Thailand May Soon Force Us to Take Out Travel Insurance Before We Holiday There." *News.Com.Au.* July 2, 2019. https://www.news.com.au/travel/travel-updates/health-safety/thailand-may-soon-force-us-to-take-out-travel-insurance-before-we-holiday-there/news-story/1049dbe8493a9f20f85cd01257f94509.

McGinley, Jennifer. "Can Gratitude Improve Quality of Life?" *Princetonhcs.org.* November 22, 2022. https://www.princetonhcs.org/about-princeton-health/news-and-information/news/can-gratitude-increase-quality-of-life#:~:text=%E2%80%94When%20gratitude%20is%20expressed%20and.

Miller, Michael. "Getting Unstuck: The Power of Naming Emotions." *Six Seconds*. January 8, 2021. www.6seconds.org/2021/01/08/getting-unstuck-power
-naming-emotions/.

Milton, Carolyn Centeno. "Fear Shrinks Your Brain and Makes You Less Creative." *Forbes*. April 18, 2018. Accessed February 16, 2024. www.forbes.com
/sites/carolyncenteno/2018/04/18/fear-shrinks-your-brain-and-makes-you
-less-creative/?sh=705182881c6d.

Moriarty, Colleen. "Having a Quarter-Life Crisis? How to Make Life Better for Future You." *Yale Medicine*. March 6, 2019. https://www.yalemedicine.org
/news/quarter-life-crisis-health#:~:text=Like%20the%20better%2D
known%20midlife.

Neill, James. "What Is Locus of Control?" 2022. https://www.usmcu.edu/Portals
/218/What%20is%20Locus%20of%20Control%20by%20James%20Neill
.pdf.

Owens, Alexandra. 2021. "Oxytocin: What It Is, How It Makes You Feel & Why It Matters." *Psycom*. September 23, 2021. https://www.psycom.net
/oxytocin.

Pidgeon, Emily. "Australian Tourists Are Hospitalised or Die Overseas Every 2.5 Hours." *Mail Online*. April 11, 2018. Accessed February 24, 2024. www
.dailymail.co.uk/news/article-5603947/Australian-tourists-hospitalised-die
-overseas-2-5-hours-worst-countries-revealed.html.

Psychpage. "List of Feeling Words." *Psychpage.com*. 2019. www.psychpage.com
/learning/library/assess/feelings.html.

Radparvar, Dave. "Neurons That Fire Together, Wire Together." *Holstee*. N.d. https://www.holstee.com/blogs/mindful-matter/neurons-that-fire-together
-wire-together.

Raypole, Crystal. "How to Increase Endorphins: 13 Tips." *Healthline*. September 27, 2019. https://www.healthline.com/health/how-to-increase
-endorphins.

Raypole, Crystal. 2020a. "12 Ways to Boost Oxytocin Naturally." *Healthline*. May 27, 2020. https://www.healthline.com/health/how-to-increase
-oxytocin#takeaway.

Raypole, Crystal. 2020b. "How to Rewire Your Brain: 6 Neuroplasticity Exercises." *Healthline*. June 17, 2020. https://www.healthline.com/health/rewiring
-your-brain#:~:text=%E2%80%9CNeuroplasticity%E2%80%9D%20
refers%20to%20your%20brain.

Raypole, Crystal, and Molly Burford. "How to Increase Serotonin: 11 Ways to Raise Serotonin Levels Naturally." *Healthline*. September 13, 2022. https://
www.healthline.com/health/how-to-increase-serotonin#manage-stress.

Robbins, Tony. "A Quote from Awaken the Giant Within." *goodreads.com*. N.d. https://www.goodreads.com/quotes/7663035-the-quality-of-your-life-is-a-direct-reflection-of.

Sevilla, Christina. "Your Brain Is like a Sledding Hill." *Colorado Community Media*. March 24, 2013. https://coloradocommunitymedia.com/stories/your-brain-is-like-a-sledding-hill.

Suttie, Jill. "Does Venting Your Feelings Actually Help?" *Greater Good*. June 21, 2021. https://greatergood.berkeley.edu/article/item/does_venting_your_feelings_actually_help.

Sutton, Jeremy. "5 Benefits of Journaling for Mental Health." *Positive-Psychology*. May 14, 2018. https://positivepsychology.com/benefits-of-journaling/.

Torre, Jared B., and Matthew D. Lieberman. "Putting Feelings into Words: Affect Labeling as Implicit Emotion Regulation." *Emotion Review* 10, no. 2 (March 2018): 116–24. https://doi.org/10.1177/1754073917742706.

University of Rochester Medical Center. "Journaling for Mental Health." *Rochester.edu*. 2019. https://www.urmc.rochester.edu/encyclopedia/content.aspx?ContentID=4552&ContentTypeID=1.

Uvnäs-Moberg, Kerstin, and Maria Petersson. "Oxytocin, a Mediator of Anti-Stress, Well-Being, Social Interaction, Growth and Healing." *Zeitschrift Für Psychosomatische Medizin Und Psychotherapie* 51, no. 1 (July 2015): 57–80. https://doi.org/10.13109/zptm.2005.51.1.57.

Vallejo, Michael. 2022. "Automatic Negative Thoughts (ANTs): How to Identify and Fix Them." *Mental Health Center Kids*. October 27, 2022. https://mentalhealthcenterkids.com/blogs/articles/automatic-negative-thoughts#:~:text=Automatic%20negative%20thoughts%20are%20a.

"Viktor E. Frankl Quotes (Author of Man's Search for Meaning)." *goodreads.com*. 2019. https://www.goodreads.com/author/quotes/2782.Viktor_E_Frankl.

Wadlinger, Heather A., and Derek M. Isaacowitz. "Positive Mood Broadens Visual Attention to Positive Stimuli." *Motivation and Emotion* 30, no. 1 (June 2006): 87–99. https://doi.org/10.1007/s11031-006-9021-1.

Whiteman, Honor. "Laughter Releases 'Feel Good Hormones' to Promote Social Bonding." *Medical News Today*. June 3, 2017. https://www.medicalnewstoday.com/articles/317756#Endorphins-might-promote-feelings-of-togetherness.

"Why Journalling Is Great for Improving Your Mood and Your Memory—and Tips to Get Started." *Vybey*. June 30, 2022. https://vybey.co.uk/blogs/vybey-blogs/why-journalling-is-great-for-improving-your-mood-and-your-memory-and-tips-to-get-started.

Wilson Jr., Robert Evans. "Are Negative Core Beliefs Wrecking Your Life?" *Psychology Today*. September 13, 2021. https://www.psychologytoday.com /us/blog/the-main-ingredient/202109/are-negative-core-beliefs-wrecking -your-life.

Wolf, Jonathan. "Later in Life, People Regret Things They Didn't Do and Failure to Become Better Versions of Themselves." *Above the Law*. March 30, 2022. https://abovethelaw.com/2022/03/later-in-life-people -regret-things-they-didnt-do-and-failure-to-become-better-versions-of -themselves/.

INDEX